高职高专机械设计与制造专业规划教材

机电与数控专业英语

石金艳　谢永超　主　编
范芳洪　副主编

清华大学出版社
北　京

内 容 简 介

本书主要介绍了机电技术专业与数控技术专业有关的专业英语知识，本书内容紧密结合专业知识，行文流畅，具有较强的趣味性，可起到巩固专业课教学内容的作用。全书共分 12 个单元，内容包括工程制图、机械零件、工程材料及其性能、机构的设计与选用、数字控制、数控操作、机床、计算机辅助设计、计算机辅助制造与柔性制造系统、计算机集成制造系统、非传统加工工艺和对话练习。为了训练学习者的英语阅读能力以及对英语文章信息的获取能力，各单元均有一定数量的配套习题。此外，每个单元还配有参考译文便于学习者的学习。

本书可作为高等职业院校机电一体化类专业、数控技术应用类专业的教材，也可作为机械制造及自动化领域相关技术人员的自学参考用书，同时还可以作为成人教育或培训班的培训用书。

本书封面贴有清华大学出版社防伪标签，无标签者不得销售。
版权所有，侵权必究。举报：010-62782989，beiqinquan@tup.tsinghua.edu.cn。

图书在版编目(CIP)数据

机电与数控专业英语/石金艳主编. —北京：清华大学出版社，2014(2023.8 重印)
(高职高专机械设计与制造专业规划教材)
ISBN 978-7-302-34875-7

Ⅰ. ①机… Ⅱ. ①石… Ⅲ. ①机电工程—英语—高等职业教育—教材 ②数控机床—加工—英语—高等职业教育—教材 Ⅳ. ①H31

中国版本图书馆 CIP 数据核字(2013)第 310937 号

责任编辑：李玉萍　桑任松
封面设计：杨玉兰
责任校对：周剑云
责任印制：刘海龙

出版发行：清华大学出版社
　　　　　网　　址：http://www.tup.com.cn，http://www.wqbook.com
　　　　　地　　址：北京清华大学学研大厦 A 座　　邮　　编：100084
　　　　　社 总 机：010-83470000　　　　　　　　　邮　　购：010-62786544
　　　　　投稿与读者服务：010-62776969，c-service@tup.tsinghua.edu.cn
　　　　　质量反馈：010-62772015，zhiliang@tup.tsinghua.edu.cn
　　　　　课件下载：http://www.tup.com.cn，010-62791865
印 装 者：北京建宏印刷有限公司
经　　销：全国新华书店
开　　本：185mm×260mm　　印　张：9.75　　字　数：235 千字
版　　次：2014 年 2 月第 1 版　　　　　　　　印　次：2023 年 8 月第 5 次印刷
印　　数：4401～4500
定　　价：32.00 元

产品编号：049631-02

前　　言

随着我国机械装备制造业的迅速发展，中国机械装备制造业在世界范围内的影响越来越广泛，中国与世界的技术交流越来越紧密。因此，掌握一定的专业英语知识，提升专业英语阅读能力，对学习国际先进的机械制造、数控加工技术等有着举足轻重的作用。

作为高职院校的一门课程，专业英语课程同其他课程一样，也要注重实践性和应用性。本书在编写过程中，主要体现以下特色。

(1) 紧跟新技术的发展，介绍了现代制造业中的一些较新技术，例如，CAD/CAM/FMS/CIMS，以反映内容的先进性。

(2) 理论联系实践，多介绍方法和案例，如机械零件、工程材料、数控操作、非传统加工工艺等内容是为工程技术人员在实践工作中随手查阅而备，使本书更具实用性。

(3) 本书采用大量图表，图文并茂，便于读者理解记忆。

(4) 本书共有 12 个单元，分别介绍了机电一体化专业、数控技术应用专业的重点知识，便于各类学校根据不同专业侧重点加以灵活选用。

(5) 本书每个单元均有大量配套的练习题及一篇与主题紧密关联的专业阅读文章。通过练习题，可以提高学习者对专业英语信息的获取能力；通过专业阅读的训练，能够提升学习者的快速阅读能力。此外，本书还对每个单元中一些典型的难句、长句进行了分析讲解，有助于学习者掌握一些专业英语的翻译技巧。

本书由湖南铁道职业技术学院石金艳、谢永超担任主编，范芳洪担任副主编。

本书在编写过程中，参考了相关的著作及资料，同时也得到了很多专家、学者的热情帮助，在此一并表示衷心感谢。

本书虽经过多次校对，但因时间仓促，加上编者水平有限，书中难免存在不足之处，恳请广大师生和读者批评指正！

编　者

目 录

Unit 1　Engineering Drawing 1
   1.1　Coordinate System 1
   1.2　Types of Views 1
   1.3　Fits 3
   Words and Expressions 5
   Notes 6
   Exercises 7
   课文参考译文 8
      第 1 单元　工程制图 8
   Technical Reading 11

Unit 2　Mechanical Components 13
   2.1　Shafts 13
   2.2　Shaft Attachments 13
   2.3　Clutches 14
   2.4　Screws 15
   2.5　Springs 15
   2.6　Gears 16
   2.7　Couplings 17
   2.8　Seals 18
   2.9　Rolling Contact Bearings 19
   Words and Expressions 20
   Notes 21
   Exercises 23
   课文参考译文 25
      第 2 单元　机械零件 25
   Technical Reading 31

Unit 3　Engineering Materials and Their Properties 32
   3.1　Engineering Materials 32
   3.2　Properties of Materials 33
   Words and Expressions 33
   Notes 34

   Exercises 35
   课文参考译文 37
      第 3 单元　工程材料及其性能 37
   Technical Reading 39

Unit 4　The Design and Selection of Mechanism Systems 40
   4.1　Design of Mechanism Systems 40
   4.2　Selection of Mechanisms 42
   Words and Expressions 45
   Notes 46
   Exercises 47
   课文参考译文 48
      第 4 单元　机构系统的设计与选用 ... 48
   Technical Reading 53

Unit 5　Numerical Control 55
   5.1　Introduction 55
   5.2　Principles of NC Machines 56
   5.3　Types of Control Systems 57
   5.4　Computer Numerical Control 57
   5.5　Advantages and Disadvantages of NC ... 58
   Words and Expressions 59
   Notes 59
   Exercises 61
   课文参考译文 62
      第 5 单元　数字控制 62
   Technical Reading 65

Unit 6　NC Operation 67
   6.1　Describing the Operation Panel 67
   6.2　Screen Reading 72
   Words and Expressions 74
   Notes 75

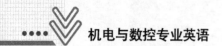

  Exercises 76
  课文参考译文 77
    第 6 单元 数控操作 77
  Technical Reading 84
    Program Input and Output 84

Unit 7 Machine Tools 86

  7.1 Lathes and Lathe Operations 86
  7.2 Milling Machine and Milling 88
  7.3 Machining Center 90
  Words and Expressions 91
  Notes 91
  Exercises 92
  课文参考译文 94
    第 7 单元 机床 94
  Technical Reading 98

Unit 8 Computer Aided Design 100

  8.1 CAD System's Work 100
  8.2 Exchange Specifications 100
  8.3 Elements of CAD System 101
  Words and Expressions 102
  Notes 103
  Exercises 103
  课文参考译文 104
    第 8 单元 计算机辅助设计 104
  Technical Reading 106

Unit 9 Computer Aided Manufacturing and Flexible Manufacturing System 109

  9.1 Computer Aided Manufacturing 109
  9.2 Flexible Manufacturing System 110
  Words and Expressions 112
  Notes 112
  Exercises 113
  课文参考译文 115
    第 9 单元 计算机辅助制造与柔性制造系统 115
  Technical Reading 117

Unit 10 Computer-integrated Manufacturing Systems 119

  10.1 Introduction 119
  10.2 Subsystems of CIM 119
  10.3 Database 121
  10.4 The CIM Wheel 122
  Words and Expressions 123
  Notes 123
  Exercises 124
  课文参考译文 126
    第 10 单元 计算机集成制造系统 ... 126
  Technical Reading 129

Unit 11 Nontraditional Machining Processes 132

  11.1 Electrical Discharge Machining 132
  11.2 Electrochemical Machining 133
  11.3 Ultrasonic Machining 133
  11.4 Laser Beam Machining 133
  11.5 Development Trends in the Field of Machining by Cutting and by Erosion ... 134
  Words and Expressions 134
  Notes 135
  Exercises 136
  课文参考译文 138
    第 11 单元 非传统加工工艺 138
  Technical Reading 140

Unit 12 Dialogue Practice 141

  12.1 Outside the Exhibition Hall 141
  12.2 Inside the Exhibition Hall 141
  12.3 In the Negotiation Booth 142
  Words and Expressions 142
  Notes 143
  Exercises 144
  课文参考译文 145
    第 12 单元 对话练习 145
  Technical Reading 147

参考文献 149

Unit 1 Engineering Drawing

The graphics are important media carrying the information to communicate, as the written words, voice, images do. Engineering drawing mainly based on graphics is the main tool used to express the design ideas in engineering design, manufacturing and construction process, known as "the language of engineering".

1.1 Coordinate System

In engineering drawing, the coordinate system is very important. The basic of all inputs in AutoCAD is the Cartesian coordinate system, and the various input (absolute or relative) rely on this system. In addition, AutoCAD has two internal coordinate systems to help you keep track of where you are in a drawing: the World Coordinate System (WCS) and the User Coordinate System (UCS).

The fixed Cartesian coordinate system locates all points on an AutoCAD drawing by defining a series of positive and negative axes to locate positions in space. Figure 1-1(a) illustrates the axes for two-dimension (2D) drafting. There is a permanent origin point (0,0) which is referenced, an x axis running horizontally in a positive and negative direction from the origin, and a y axis traveling perpendicularly in a vertical direction. When a point is located, it is based on the origin point unless you are working in the three dimension, in which case you will have a third axis, called the z axis (see Fig. 1-1(b)).

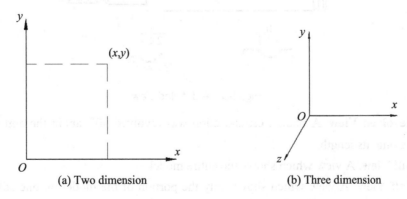

Fig. 1-1 The coordinate system

1.2 Types of Views

Many types of views are used to express the design ideas in engineering design in the area of Engineering drawing.

(1) **Projection View**. An orthographic projection of an object as seen from the front, top,

right side, etc, as illustrated in Fig. 1-2. Fig. 1-2 (a) is the object, and Fig. 1-2 (b) is the orthographic projection of the object.

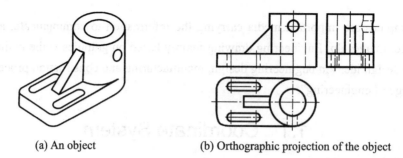

(a) An object   (b) Orthographic projection of the object

Fig. 1-2 An orthographic projection of an object

(2) **Auxiliary View**. Any view created by projecting 90° to an inclined surface, datum plane, or along an axis.

(3) **General View**. Any view which is oriented by the user and is not dependent on any other view for its orientation.

(4) **Detailed View**. Any view which is derived by taking a portion of an existing view and scaling it for the purpose of dimensioning and clarification. The following Fig. 1-3 is a typical example of detailed view. There are two detailed views in Fig. 1-3, that is, I and II.

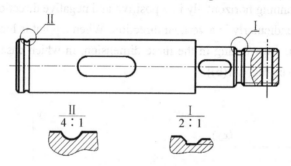

Fig. 1-3 A detailed view

(5) **Revolved View**. A planar, cross-section was revolved 90° about the cutting plane line and offset along, its length.

(6) **Full View**. A view which shows the entire model.

(7) **Half View**. A view which shows only the portion of the model on one side of a datum plane.

(8) **Broken View**. Used on large objects to remove a section between two points and move the remaining section close together.

(9) **Section View**. A view which displays a cross-section for a particular view, as shown in Fig. 1-4.

(10) **Exploded View**. The exploded view is a type of pictorial drawing designed to show several parts in their proper location prior to assembly. Although the exploded view is not used as

the working drawing for the machinist, it has an important place in mechanical technology. Exploded views appear extensively in manuals and handbooks that are used for repair and assembly of machines and other mechanisms.

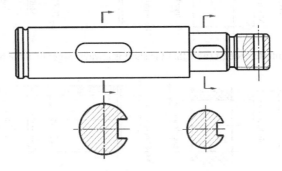

Fig. 1-4 A section view

(11) **Partial View**. When a symmetrical object is drafted, two views are sufficient to represent it (typically, one view is omitted). A partial view can be used to substitute one of the two views. Section and auxiliary views are also commonly used to present part detail. Section views are extremely useful in displaying the detailed design of a complicated internal configuration. If the section is symmetrical around a centerline, only the upper half needs to be shown. The lower half is typically shown only in outline. Casting designers often employ section views to explode detail. When a major surface is inclined to three projection planes, only a distorted picture can be seen. An auxiliary plane that is parallel to the major surface can be used to display an undistorted view.

1.3 Fits

The fit between two mating parts is the relationship which results from the clearance or interference obtained. There are three classes of fits, namely, clearance, transition and interference. These conditions are shown in the following Fig. 1-5.

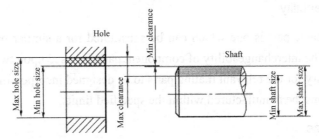

(a) Clearance fit (note that the shaft is always smaller than the hole)

Fig. 1-5 Classes of fits between a hole and a shaft

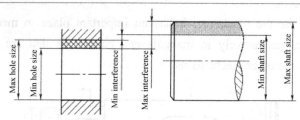

(b) Interference fit (note that the shaft is always larger than the hole)

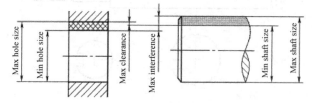

(c) Transition fit (note that the limits are such that the condition may be of clearance or interference fit)

Fig. 1-5　Classes of fits between a hole and a shaft(continued)

The following Fig. 1-6 is a typical example of the dimensioning of fit code in the assembly drawing.

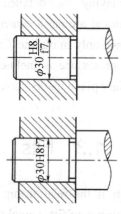

Fig. 1-6　A typical example of the dimensioning of fit code in the assembly drawing

1. Interchangeability

An interchangeable part is one which can be substituted for a similar part manufactured to the same drawing. The interchangeability of component parts is based upon two functions:

(1) It is necessary for the relevant mating parts to be designed incorporating limits of size.

(2) The parts must be manufactured within the specified limits.

2. Limits of Size

In deciding the limits necessary for a particular dimension, there are three consideration: functional importance, interchangeability and economics. The first necessitates a knowledge of what the component is required to do, the second its replacement in the event of failure, and the third the avoidance of unnecessary time and money being spent in production. The decision as to the degree of tolerance that can be utilized calls for discretion in the compromise between accuracy and economy. In order to assist the designer in his choice of limits and fits and to encourage uniformity throughout industry (home and abroad), a number of limit-and-fit systems have been published.

Words and Expressions

coordinate [kəu'ɔ:dineit]	坐标，坐标系
coordinate system	坐标系
coordinate value	坐标值
Cartesian [kɑ:'ti:ziən]	笛卡儿
Cartesian coordinate system	笛卡儿坐标系
keep track of	跟踪定位于
World Coordinate System (WCS)	世界坐标系
User Coordinate System (UCS)	用户坐标系
perpendicularly [ˌpə:pən'dikjuləli]	与……垂直
projection [prə'dʒekʃən]	投影，计划，设计
orthographic projection	正交投影
projection drawing	投影图
projection plane	投影面
projection method	投影法
inclined surface	斜面
inclination [ˌinkli'neiʃən]	倾斜，斜度，倾角
datum plane	基准面
datum dimension	基准标注
general drawing	总图
detail ['di:teil]	局部放大图
planar ['pleinə]	平面的，二维的
planar graph	平面图
planar construction	平面结构
offset ['ɔfˌset]	偏置，偏移
partial ['pɑ:ʃəl]	局部的，图示的
partial view	局部视图
exploded view	分解图，爆炸图
symmetrical [si'metrikəl]	对称的
asymmetrical [ˌeisi'metrikl]	不对称的
section view	剖视图，剖面图
mate [meit]	配合
orient ['ɔ:riənt]	定向，定位

orienting line		基线
orienting point		基点
clearance	['klɪərəns]	间隙
transition	[træn'zɪʃn]	过渡
interference	[ˌɪntə'fɪərəns]	过盈

Notes

(1) The basic of all inputs in AutoCAD is the Cartesian coordinate system, and the various inputs (absolute or relative) rely on this system.

The basic of … 在此的意思是"……的基础"，rely on 的意思是"依赖，依靠"。

本句可以翻译为：笛卡儿坐标系是 AutoCAD 中所有输入的基础，各种输入方法(如绝对坐标、相对坐标)都依赖于这个系统。

(2) When a point is located, it is based on the origin point unless you are working in the three dimension, in which case you will have a third axis, called the z axis.

unless 引导让步状语从句，in which case 引导的从句在此作定语修饰 dimension，called the z axis 在此作为 third axis 的后置定语。

本句可以翻译为：根据原点(0,0)标记其他任意一个点，但是在三维空间中绘图时，应该有第三根轴，称为 z 轴。

(3) Section and auxiliary views are also commonly used to present part detail.

to present part detail 作目的状语。

本句可以翻译为：剖面图和辅助视图也经常用于表达零件细节。

(4) An interchangeable part is one which can be substituted for a similar part manufactured to the same drawing.

interchangeable 在此为动词 interchange 的形容词形式，翻译为"可以互换的，可交换的"。

substitute for 在此意思是"代替，替换，取代"。

本句可以翻译为：可互换的零件是一种能由同一图纸加工出来的相似零件所代替的零件。

(5) In deciding the limits necessary for a particular dimension, there are three consideration: functional importance, interchangeability and economics.

本句可以翻译为：对一个具体尺寸给定公差带时，需要考虑三个方面：功能重要性、可互换性和经济性。

Exercises

1. Answer the following questions according to the text above.

   (1) What is the Cartesian coordinate system and its function?
   (2) How many types of views are there according to our text? Give their names.
   (3) What is the detailed view and its function?
   (4) How many types of fits are there according to our text? Give their names.
   (5) What needs to be considered while deciding the limits necessary for a particular dimension?

2. Fill in the blanks with proper words or phrases according to the text (note the proper tense).

   (1) AutoCAD has two internal coordinate systems, they are _____ and _____.
   (2) There are many types of views in the text, namely_____, _____, _____, _____, _____, _____, _____, _____, and_____.
   (3) There are three classes of fits, namely_____, _____, and_____.

3. Translate the following expressions into Chinese.

   (1) Coordinate system
   (2) Cartesian coordinate system
   (3) Keep track of
   (4) World Coordinate System (WCS)
   (5) User Coordinate System (UCS)
   (6) Orthographic projection
   (7) Projection plane
   (8) Partial View
   (9) Degree of tolerance
   (10) Home and abroad

4. Translate the following sentences into Chinese.

   (1) AutoCAD has two internal coordinate systems to help you keep track of where you are in a drawing: the World Coordinate System (WCS) and the User Coordinate System (UCS).

   (2) The fixed Cartesian coordinate system locates all points on an AutoCAD drawing by defining a series of positive and negative axes to locate positions in space.

   (3) There is a permanent origin point (0,0) which is referenced, an x axis running horizontally in a positive and negative direction from the origin, and a y axis traveling

perpendicularly in a vertical direction.

(4) The first necessitates a knowledge of what the component is required to do, the second its replacement in the event of failure, and the third the avoidance of unnecessary time and money being spent in production.

5. Write a 100-word summary according to the text.

课文参考译文

第1单元 工程制图

图形和文字、声音、图像一样，是承载信息进行交流的重要媒体。以图形为主的工程图样是工程设计、制造和施工过程中用来表达设计思想的主要工具，被称为"工程界的语言"。

1.1 坐标系

在工程制图中，坐标系是十分重要的。笛卡儿坐标系是 AutoCAD 中所有输入的基础，各种输入方法(如绝对坐标、相对坐标)都依赖于这个系统。此外，AutoCAD 有两个内部坐标系：世界坐标系(WCS)和用户坐标系(UCS)，用来帮助确定你在绘图区中的位置。

固定的笛卡儿坐标系可以通过定义一系列用以确定空间位置的正负轴来标记 AutoCAD 图上的所有点。图 1-1(a)所示为二维绘图的坐标系。坐标系有一个作为参考点的固定原点(0,0)，x 轴从原点出发沿着水平方向向左右延伸，y 轴从原点出发沿着垂直方向上下延伸。根据原点(0,0)标记其他任意一个点，但是在三维空间中绘图时，应该有第三根轴，称为 z 轴，如图 1-1(b)所示。

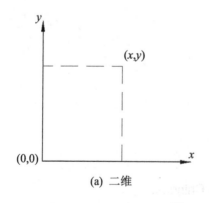

图 1-1 坐标系

1.2 视图类型

在工程制图领域，采用各种视图类型来表达机械设计的设计理念。

(1) **投影视图**——是从前面、顶面、右侧面等方向观察物体的正交投影图，如图 1-2 所示。图 1-2(a)为物体的实物图，图 1-2(b)为物体的正交投影图。

(2) **辅助视图**——向倾斜面、参考面或沿着一个轴线作 90°投影所产生的视图。

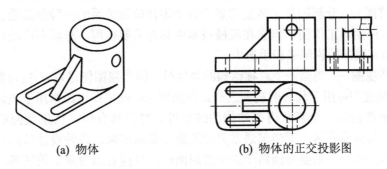

(a) 物体　　　　　　　　　(b) 物体的正交投影图

图 1-2　一个物体的正交投影

(3) **总图**——由用户确定位置，并且其定向不依赖于其他定位视图的视图。

(4) **局部放大图**——为了标注尺寸和看清图形而从已知视图中取出一部分并将其放大的一种视图。图 1-3 是一幅局部放大图的典型例子。图 1-3 中有两处用到了局部放大图，分别为Ⅰ处和Ⅱ处。

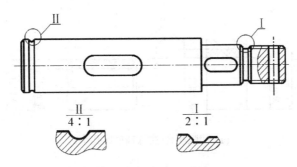

图 1-3　局部放大图的典型例子

(5) **旋转视图**——二维平面中，横截面绕剖切线旋转 90°后移出一定距离的视图。

(6) **全视图**——显示整个模型的视图。

(7) **半视图**——只显示在参考面一侧的部分图形。

(8) **折断视图**——用于表达大的物体，移去(中间)两点间的一段截面并把剩余部分移到一起的截面视图。

(9) **剖面图**　用于显示某个视图的横截面，如图 1-4 所示。

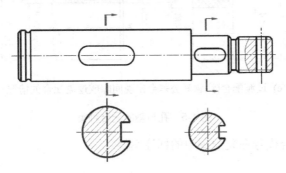

图 1-4　剖面图

(10) 分解图——分解图是在装配前显示每个零件位置关系的一种示意图。尽管机械师不把部件分解图用作工作图，但它在机械技术中具有重要作用。分解图广泛出现在机器或机械装置维修和装配的说明书和手册中。

(11) 局部视图——当画一个对称结构的物体时，两个视图便足以表达(习惯上一个视图被省略)。局部视图可用于代替两视图之一。剖面图和辅助视图也经常用于表达零件的局部细节。剖面图在显示一个复杂内部结构的细节设计时尤其有用。如果截面沿着中心线对称，只有上半部需要表达。下半部通常只用轮廓线显示出来。铸件设计师们通常利用截面图来分解局部。当一个主要面倾斜于三个投影面时，只能看到歪曲了的图形，一个平行于该主要面的辅助平面，可用来显示物体未被歪曲的视图。

1.3 配合

两个相互匹配的零件之间的配合是一种由间隙或过盈导出的关系。配合有三种类型，即间隙配合、过渡配合和过盈配合，如图 1-5 所示。

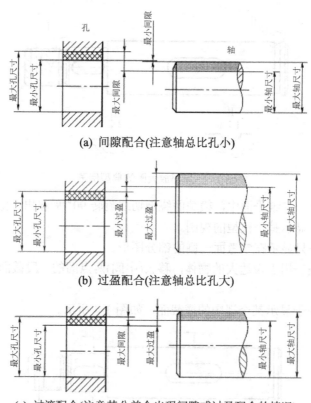

(a) 间隙配合(注意轴总比孔小)

(b) 过盈配合(注意轴总比孔大)

(c) 过渡配合(注意其公差会出现间隙或过盈配合的情况)

图 1-5 孔与轴的配合种类

图 1-6 所示为配合代号在装配图中的标注案例。

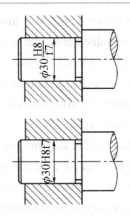

图 1-6 配合代号在装配图中的标注案例

1. 可互换性

可互换的零件是一种能由同一图纸加工出来的相似零件所代替的零件。零件的互换性要基于两个功能。

(1) 对于相互配合的零件来说，设计成融合的尺寸公差是十分必要的。

(2) 必须在指定的公差内制造零件。

2. 尺寸公差

对一个具体尺寸给定公差带时，需要考虑三个方面：功能重要性、可互换性和经济性。第一，有必要了解这个元件的用途；第二，要了解失效场合下它的替换性；第三，要考虑避免在生产上花费不必要的时间和金钱。至于决定采用何种可行的公差等级，则要在精确性与经济性之间评判协调。为帮助设计者选择公差与配合以及鼓励整个工业界的一致性(国内和国外)，已经发布了许多公差与配合系统。

Technical Reading

Dimension and Tolerance

In deciding a drawing, the numbers placed in the dimension lines represent dimensions that are only approximate and do not represent any degrees of accuracy unless so stated by the designer. The numbers are termed as nominal size. The nominal size of a component dimension is arrived at as a convenient size based on the design process. However, it is almost impossible to produce any component to the exact dimension through any of the known manufacturing processes. Even if a component is perceived to be made to the exact dimension by manual process, the actual measurement with a high resolution measuring device will show that this is an incorrect perception. It is therefore customary in engineering practice to allow a permissible deviation from the nominal size, which is termed as tolerance. Tolerance on a dimension can also specify the degree of accuracy. For example, a shaft might have a nominal size of 53.5 mm. If a variation of ±0.06 mm could be permitted, the dimension would be stated 53.5±0.06 mm.

In engineering, when a product is designed, it consists of a number of parts and these parts mate with each other in some form. In the assembly, it is important to consider the type of mating or fit between two parts which will actually define the way the parts are to behave during the working of the assembly. Take for example a shaft and hole, which will have to fit together. In the simplest case, if the dimension of the shaft is lower than the dimension of the hole, then there will be clearance. Such a fit is termed clearance fit. Alternatively, if the dimension of the shaft is more than that of the hole, then it is termed interference fit.

Dimensions given close tolerances means that the part must fit properly with some other parts. Both must be given tolerances in keeping with the allowance desired, the manufacturing processes available, and the minimum cost of production and assembly that will maximize profit. Generally speaking, the cost of a part goes up as the tolerance is decreased. If a part has several or more surfaces to be machined, the cost can be excessive when little deviation is allowed from the nominal size.

Allowance, which is sometimes confused with tolerance, has an altogether different meaning. It is the minimum clearance space intended between mating parts and represents the condition of the tightest permissible fit. If a shaft, size $1.498 _{-0.003}^{-0.000}$, is to fit a hole of size $1.500 _{-0.000}^{+0.003}$, the minimum size hole is 1.500 and the maximum size shaft is 1.498. Thus the allowance is 0.002 and the maximum clearance is 0.008 as based on the minimum shaft size and maximum hole dimension.

Tolerances may be either unilateral or bilateral. Unilateral tolerance means that any variation is made in only one direction from the nominal or basic dimension. Referring to the previous example, the hole is dimensioned $1.500 _{-0.000}^{+0.003}$, which represents a unilateral tolerance. Here the nominal size 1.500 is allowed to vary between 1.503 and 1.5. If the dimension were given as 1.5±0.003, the tolerance would be bilateral. That is, it would vary both over and under the nominal dimension. In bilateral tolerance the variation of the limits can be uniformed as 30.00±0.02. The dimension varies from 30.02 to 29.98. Alternatively the allowed deviation can be different as $30 _{-0.10}^{+0.05}$. Here the dimension varies from 30.05 to 29.90. Sometimes the nominal size may be outside the allowable limits. For example, a given dimension is to vary from 29.95 to 29.85. It can be written as $29.95 _{-0.10}^{+0}$ or $30 _{-0.15}^{-0.05}$. The second form is preferred since it contains the nominal size 30. The unilateral system permits changing the tolerance while still retaining the same allowance or type of fit. With the bilateral system, it is not possible without changing the nominal size dimension of one or both of the two mating parts. In mass production, where mating parts must be interchangeable, unilateral tolerances are customary. To have an interference or force fit between mating parts, the tolerances must be such as to create a zero or negative allowance.

Unit 2 Mechanical Components

The machine plays an important role in the mechanical industrial production. Mechanical components are the basic elements to form a machine. This unit describes commonly used mechanical components, such as shafts, shaft attachments, clutches, screws, springs, gears, couplings, seals and rolling contact bearings.

2.1 Shafts

1. Solid Shafts

As a machine component, a shaft is commonly a cylindrical bar that supports and rotates with devices for receiving and delivering rotary motion and torque. Figure 2-1 illustrates a typical stepped shaft.

2. Flexible Shafts

Compared with solid shafts, flexible shafts can be bent too much smaller radii without being overstressed.

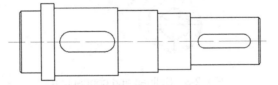

Fig. 2-1 A stepped shaft

2.2 Shaft Attachments

The primary purpose of keys, splines and pins is to prevent relative rotary movement.

1. Keys

A key is the machinery component placed at the interface between a shaft and the hub of a power-transmitting element for the purpose of transmitting torque (see Fig. 2-2(a)). The key is demountable to facilitate assembly and disassembly of the shaft system. It is installed in an axial groove machined into the shaft, called a keyseat. A similar groove in the hub of the power-transmitting element is usually called a keyway, but it is more properly called a keyseat. The key is typically installed into the shaft keyseat first; then the hub keyseat is aligned with the key, and the hub is slid into position.

The most common type of key for shafts up to 6.5 inches in diameter is the square key, as illustrated in Fig. 2-2(b). The rectangular key (illustrated in Fig. 2-2(c)) is recommended for larger shafts and is used for smaller shafts where the shorter height can be tolerated. Both the square and the rectangular keys are referred to as parallel keys because the top, bottom and the sides of the key are parallel.

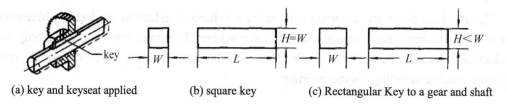

(a) key and keyseat applied (b) square key (c) Rectangular Key to a gear and shaft

Fig. 2-2 Parallel keys

The keyseats in the shaft and the hub are designed so that exactly one-half of the height of the key is bearing on the side of the shaft keyseat and the other half on the side of the hub keyseat.

2. Splines

Splines are permanent keys integral with the shaft, fitting in keyways cut in the hub. The dimensions of spline fittings are standardized for both permanent (press) fits and sliding fits (see Fig. 2-3).

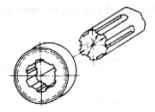

Fig. 2-3 Splines and connection

3. Pins

Tapered circular pins can be used to restrain shaft-mounted members from both axial and rotational movement (see Fig. 2-4).

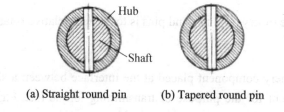

(a) Straight round pin (b) Tapered round pin

Fig. 2-4 Pins for torque transmission and component location

2.3 Clutches

A clutch (see Fig. 2-5) is a device for quickly and easily connecting or disconnecting a rotary shaft with a rotating coaxial shaft. Clutches are usually placed between the input shaft to a machine and the output shaft from the driving motor, and provide a convenient means for starting and stopping the machine and permitting the driver or engine to be started in an unloaded state.

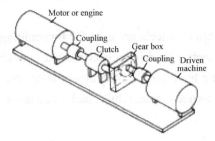

Fig. 2-5 Typical applications of clutches

2.4 Screws

Screws have been used as fastener for a long time; a screw consists of a circular cylinder (or truncated cone) with a helical groove in it.

Screws with screwdriver slots have heads of several shapes, such as flat, oval and round.

Screws with hexagonal heads are usually known as cap screws. These screws are used to clamp machine parts together when one of the parts has an internal thread. If neither parts is threaded a bolt must be used, which consists of a screw with a hexagonal head, a nut (hexagonal ring with an internal thread), and usually a washer (flat ring).

2.5 Springs

A spring is a load-sensitive, energy-storing device, the chief characteristics of which are an ability to tolerate large deflections without failure and to recover its initial size and shape when loads are removed.

Springs are used for a variety of purposes, such as supplying the motive power in clocks and watches, cushioning transport vehicles, measuring weights, making resilient connections, and providing shock protection for delicate instruments during shipment. Figure 2-6 illustrates the springs and spring application.

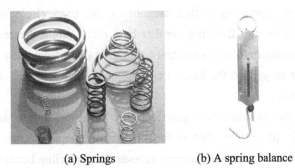

(a) Springs (b) A spring balance

Fig. 2-6 Springs and spring application

2.6 Gears

Gears are toothed. Cylindrical wheels are used for transmitting motion and power from one rotating shaft to another. The teeth of a driving gear mesh accurately in the spaces between teeth on the driven gear. The driving teeth push on the driven teeth, exerting a force perpendicular to the radius of the gear. Thus, a torque is transmitted, and because the gear is rotating, power is also transmitted.

1. Spur Gear Geometry

The most widely used spur gear tooth form is the full-depth involute form. Its characteristic shape is shown in Fig. 2-7.

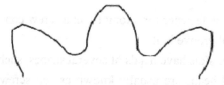

Fig. 2-7　Involute-tooth form

The involute is one of a class of geometric curves called conjugate curves. When two such gear teeth are in mesh and rotating, there is a constant angular velocity ratio between them. From the moment of initial contact to the moment of disengagement, the speed of the driving gear is in a constant proportion to the speed of the driven gear. The resulting action of the two gears is very smooth. Otherwise there would be speeding up or slowing down during the engagement, with the resulting accelerations causing vibration noise, and dangerous torsional oscillations in the system.

An involute curve can be seen by taking a cylinder and wrapping a string around its circumference. Tie a pencil to the end of the string. Then start with the pencil tight against the cylinder, and hold the string taut. Move the pencil away from the cylinder while keeping the string taut. The curve drawn is an involute.

The circle represented by the cylinder is called the base circle. Notice that at any position on the curve, the string represents a line tangent to the base circle and, at the same time, perpendicular to the involute. Drawing another base circle along the same centerline in such a position that the resulting involute is tangent to the first one, it demonstrates that at the point of contact, the two lines tangent to the base circles are coincident and will stay in the same position as the base circles rotate.

This is what happens when two gear teeth are in mesh. It is a fundamental principle of kinematics, the study of motion, that if the line drawn perpendicular to the surfaces of two rotating bodies at the point of contact always crosses the centerline between the two bodies at the same place, the angular velocity ratio of the two bodies will be constant. This is a statement of gearing. As demonstrated here, the gear teeth made in the involute-tooth form obey the law.

2. Helical Gear Geometry

Helical and spur gears are distinguished by the orientation of their teeth. On spur gears, the teeth are straight and are aligned with the axis of the gear. On helical gears, the teeth are inclined at an angle with the axis, that angle being called the helix angle. If the gear was very wide, it would appear that the teeth wind around the gear blank in a continuous, helical path. However, practical considerations limit the width of the gears so that the teeth normally appear to be merely inclined with respect to the axis. Figure 2-8 shows two examples of commercially available helical gears. The forms of helical gear teeth are very similar to those discussed for spur gears. The basic task is to account for the effect of the helix angle.

right hand helix
left hand helix

Fig. 2-8 Helical gears

2.7 Couplings

The term coupling refers to a device used to connect two shafts together at their ends for the purpose of transmitting power. There are two general types of couplings: rigid and flexible.

1. Rigid Couplings

Rigid couplings are designed to draw two shafts together tightly so that no relative motion can occur between them. This design is desirable for certain kinds of equipment in which precise alignment of two shafts is required and can be provided. In such cases, the coupling must be designed to be capable of transmitting the torque in the shafts.

A typical rigid coupling is shown in Fig. 2-9(a), in which flanges are mounted on the ends of each shaft and are drawn together by a series of bolts. The load path is then from the driving shaft to its flange, through the bolts, into the mating flange, and out to the driven shaft. The torque places the bolts in shear. The total shear force on the bolts depends on the radius of the bolt circle and the torque.

Rigid couplings should be used only when the alignment of the two shafts can be maintained very accurately, not only at the time of installation but also during operation of the machines, as Fig.2-9(a) shown. If significant angular, radial, or axial misalignment occurs, stresses that are difficult to predict and that may lead to early failure due to fatigue will be induced in the shafts. These difficulties can be overcome by the use of flexible couplings.

 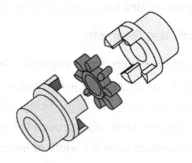

(a) A rigid coupling　　　　　　　　(b) A flexible coupling

Fig. 2-9　Couplings

2. Flexible Couplings

Flexible couplings (see Fig. 2-9(b)) are designed to transmit torque smoothly while permitting some axial, radial, and angular misalignment. The flexibility is such that when misalignment does occur, parts of the coupling move with little or no resistance. Thus, no significant axial or bending stresses are developed in the shaft. Many types of flexible couplings are available commercially. Each of them is designed to transmit a given limiting torque. The manufacturer's catalog lists the design data from which you can choose a suitable coupling. Remember that torque equals power divided by rotational speed. So for a given size of coupling, as the speed of rotation increases, the amount of power that the coupling can transmit also increases, although not always in direct proportion. Of course, centrifugal effects determine the upper limit of speed.

2.8　Seals

Seals are an important part of machine design in situations where the following conditions apply:
- Contaminants must be excluded from critical areas of a machine.
- Lubricants must be contained within a space.
- Pressurized fluids must be contained within a component such as a valve or a hydraulic cylinder.

Some of the parameters affecting the choice of the type of sealing system, the materials used, and the details of its design are as follows:
- The nature of the fluids to be contained or excluded.
- Pressures on both sides of the seal.
- The nature of any relative motion between the seal and the mating components.
- Temperatures on all parts of the sealing system.
- The degree of sealing required. Is some small amount of leakage permissible?
- The life expectancy of the system.
- The nature of the solid materials against which the seal must act: corrosion potential,

smoothness, hardness, wear resistance.
- Ease of service for replacement of worn sealing elements.

The number of designs for sealing systems is virtually limitless, and only a brief overview will be presented here. Often, designers rely on technical information provided by manufacturers of complete sealing systems or specific sealing elements. Also, in critical or unusual situations, testing of a proposed design is advised.

2.9 Rolling Contact Bearings

The purpose of a bearing is to support a load while permitting relative motion between two elements of a machine. The term rolling contact bearings refers to the wide variety of bearings that use spherical balls or some other type of roller between the stationary and the moving elements. The most common type of bearing supports a rotating shaft, resisting purely radial loads or a combination of radial and axial (thrust) loads. Some bearings are designed to carry only thrust loads. Most bearings are used in applications involving rotation, but some are used in linear motion applications.

The components of a typical rolling contact bearing are the inner race, the outer race, and the rolling elements. Figure 2-10 shows the common single-row, groove ball bearing. Usually the outer race is stationary and is held by the housing of the machine. The inner race is pressed onto the rotating shaft and thus rotates with it. Then the balls roll between the outer and inner races. The load path is from the shaft, to the inner race, to the balls, to the outer race, and finally to the housing. The presence of the balls allows a very smooth, low-friction rotation of the shaft. The typical coefficient of friction for a rolling contact bearing is approximately 0.001 to 0.005. These values reflect only the rolling elements themselves and the means of retaining them in the bearing.

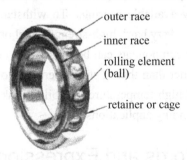

Fig. 2-10　Single-row, groove ball bearing

1. Types of Rolling Contact Bearing

Here we will discuss several different types of rolling contact bearings and the applications in which each is typically used.

Radial loads act toward the center of the bearing along a radius. Such loads are typical of those created by power transmission elements on shafts such as spur gears, V-belt drives, and chain drives. Thrust loads are those that act parallel to the axis of the shaft. The axial components of the forces on helical gears, worms and worm gears, and bevel gears are thrust loads. Also, bearings supporting shafts with vertical axes are subjected to thrust loads due to the weight of the shaft and the elements on the shaft as well as from axial operating forces. Misalignment refers to the angular deviation of the axis of the shaft at the bearing from the true axis of the bearing itself. An excellent rating form is alignment in Table 2-1 indicates that the bearing can accommodate up to 4.0° of angular deviation. A bearing with a fair rating can with stand up to 0.15°, while a poor rating indicates that rigid shafts with less than 0.05° of misalignment are required. Manufacturers' catalogs should be consulted for specific data.

Table 2-1 Comparison of bearing types

Bearing types	Radial load capacity	Thrust load capacity	Misalignment capability
Single-row, deep-groove ball	Good	Fair	Fair
Double-row, deep-groove ball	Excellent	Good	Fair
Angular contact	Good	Excellent	Poor
Cylindrical roller	Excellent	Poor	Fair
Spherical roller	Excellent	Fair/good	Excellent
Needle	Excellent	Poor	Poor
Tapered roller	Excellent	Excellent	Poor

2. Bearing Materials

The load on a rolling contact bearing is exerted on a small area. The resulting contact stresses are quite high, regardless of the type of bearing. Contact stresses of approximately 300 000 psi are not uncommon in commercially available bearings. To withstand such high stresses, the balls, rollers, and races are made from a very hard, high-strength steel or ceramic.

Rolling elements and other components can be made from ceramic materials such as silicon nitride. Although the cost is higher than that of steels, ceramics offer significant advantages. The light weight, high strength, and high temperature capability make them desirable for aerospace, engine, military, and other demanding applications.

Words and Expressions

shaft　　[ʃɑ:ft]　　　　　轴
clutch　　[klʌtʃ]　　　　离合器
key　　[ki:]　　　　　　键
hub　　[hʌb]　　　　　轮毂
pin　　[pin]　　　　　　销
involute　　['invəlju:t]　　渐开线

perpendicular [ˌpə:pən'dikjulə]	垂直的
engagement [in'geidʒmənt]	啮合
helical gear	斜齿轮
helix angle	螺旋角
contaminant [kən'tæmənənt]	杂质
leakage ['li:kidʒ]	泄漏，渗漏
retainer [ri'teinə]	保持架
axial thrust load	轴向推力载荷
flexible coupling	柔性联轴器
sealing system	密封系统
inner race	内圈
radial load	径向载荷
deep-groove ball bearing	深沟球轴承
accessory [æk'sesəri]	附件，配件
screw [skru:]	螺钉
keyseat ['ki:si:t]	键槽
spline [splain]	花键
coaxial shaft	同心轴
mesh [meʃ]	啮合
torque [tɔ:k]	扭矩
spur gear	直齿轮，正齿轮
bevel gear	锥齿轮
conjugate curves	共轭曲线
lubricant ['lu:brikənt]	润滑剂
spherical ['sferikəl]	球的，球形的
ceramic [si'ræmik]	陶瓷
rigid coupling	刚性联轴器
hydraulic cylinder	液压缸
rolling contact bearing	滚动接触轴承
outer race	外圈
axial load	轴向载荷
angular contact ball bearing	角接触球轴承

Notes

(1) A key is the machinery component placed at the interface between a shaft and the hub of a power-transmitting element for the purpose of transmitting torque.

for the purpose of 在此的意思是"目的是，为了……目的"

本句可以翻译为：键是一种置于轴与传递动力的轮毂之间的机械零件，用于传递转矩。

(2) The rectangular key (illustrated in Figure2-2 (c)) is recommended for larger shafts and is used for smaller shafts where the shorter height can be tolerated.

本句可以翻译为：对于较大的轴，推荐采用矩形键(如图 2-2(c)所示)，当高度较低的一边允许时，可用于较小的轴。

(3) A spring is a load-sensitive, energy-storing device, the chief characteristics of which are an ability to tolerate large deflections without failure and to recover its initial size and shape when loads are removed.

这是一个比较长的句子，对于这个句子，可以分为两句：即"A spring is a load-sensitive, energy-storing device, the chief characteristics of …"，which 可以用词"such a device"来代替。

本句可以翻译为：弹簧是一个对载荷敏感、可储存能量的元件，其主要特性是允许大变形而不失效，且载荷撤销后能够恢复到初始尺寸和形状。

(4) The driving teeth push on the driven teeth, exerting a force perpendicular to the radius of the gear.

driving teeth 在此翻译为"主动轮齿"，"driven teeth"在此翻译为"从动轮齿"。

本句可以翻译为：主动轮齿推动从动轮齿运动，产生一个垂直于齿轮半径的作用力。

(5) Otherwise there would be speeding up or slowing down during the engagement, with the resulting accelerations causing vibration noise, and dangerous tosional oscillations in the system.

speeding up 的意思是"加速"，slowing down 的意思是"减速"。

本句可以翻译为：否则在啮合时就会加速或减慢，产生的加速度会引起振动、噪声以及危险的扭矩震荡。

(6) It is a fundamental principle of kinematics, the study of motion, that if the line drawn perpendicular to the surfaces of two rotating bodies at the point of contact always crosses the centerline between the two bodies at the same place, the angular velocity ratio of the two bodies will be constant.

perpendicular to 指的是"垂直于"。

本句可以翻译为：运动学(研究运动)的一条基本原理是，如果在接触点垂直于两个定轴转动物体的直线总是在同一位置过两物体的中心线，则两物体的角速度保持常数。

(7) This design is desirable for certain kinds of equipment in which precise alignment of two shafts is required and can be provided.

be desirable for sth.在此翻译为"令人满意的，理想的"。

本句可以翻译为：对于某些设备而言，当两轴要求具有精确的对中性时，这种设计才是令人满意的。

(8) A typical rigid coupling is shown in Fig. 2-9(a), in which flanges are mounted on the ends of each shaft and are drawn together by a series of bolts.

be mounted on 的意思是"安装在……，安装于……之上"

本句可以翻译为：典型的刚性联轴器每根轴的末端装上凸缘并用螺栓连在一起。

(9) The term rolling contact bearings refers to the wide variety of bearings that use spherical

balls or some other type of roller between the stationary and the moving elements.

refer to 可以翻译为"指的是"。

本句可以翻译为：滚动接触轴承是指在静止元件与运动元件之间使用球或其他类型滚动体的、种类繁多的轴承。

(10) Misalignment refers to the angular deviation of the axis of the shaft at the bearing from the true axis of the bearing itself.

本句可以翻译为：偏斜是指轴在轴承上的中心线与轴承自身中心线的角度偏差。

(11) A bearing with a fair rating can with stand up to 0.15°, while a poor rating indicates that rigid shafts with less than 0.05° of misalignment are required.

本句可以翻译为：一般等级的轴承最高可以承受 0.15°的偏斜，而较差等级的则要求刚性轴的偏斜小于 0.05°。

Exercises

1. After reading the text above, summarize the main ideas in oral.

2. Fill in the blanks with proper words or phrases according to the text (note the proper tense).

(1) In this text, some commonly used mechanical components are introduced. They are _____.

(2) The key is d_____ to facilitate assembly and disassembly of the shaft system.

(3) This design is desirable for certain kinds of equipment in which precise a_____ of two shafts is required and can be provided.

(4) Often, designers r_____ technical information provided by manufacturers of complete sealing systems or specific sealing elements.

(5) Of course, c_____ determine the upper limit of speed.

(6) The term coupling r_____ a device used to connect two shafts together at their ends for the purpose of transmitting power.

3. Translate the following phrases into Chinese.

(1) be aligned with
(2) refer to
(3) depend on
(4) lead to
(5) exclude from
(6) life expectancy
(7) rigid coupling
(8) flexible coupling
(9) hydraulic cylinder

(10) sealing system

(11) load-sensitive

(12) proposed design

(13) resultant force

(14) linear motion

(15) angular deviation

(16) axial component

(17) interference fit

(18) ceramic material

4. Translate the following phrases into English.

(1) 斜齿轮

(2) 直齿轮

(3) 锥齿轮

(4) 轴向载荷

(5) 刚性联轴器

(6) 平键

(7) 相对运动

(8) 柔性联轴器

(9) 密封系统

(10) 抗磨损性

(11) 内圈

(12) 外圈

(13) 保持架

(14) 深沟球轴承

(15) 角接触轴承

(16) 接触应力

5. Write a 100-word summary according to the text.

6. Translate the passage below into Chinese.

A coupling is a device for connecting the ends of adjacent shafts. In machine construction, couplings are used to effect a semi-permanent connection between adjacent rotating shafts. The connection is permanent in the sense that it is not meant to be broken during the useful life of the machine, but it can be broken and restored in an emergency or when worn parts are replaced.

There are several types of shaft couplings; their characteristics depend on the purpose for which they are used. If an exceptionally long shaft is required for a line shaft in the manufacturing plant or a propeller shaft on ship, it is made in sections that are coupled together with rigid couplings.

In connecting shafts belonging to separate devices (such as an electrical motor and gearbox), precise aligning of the shafts is difficult and a flexible coupling is used. This coupling connects the shafts in such a way as to minimize the harmful effects of shaft misalignment. Flexible couplings also permit the shafts to defect under their separate systems of loads and to move freely (float) in the axial direction without interfering with one another. Flexible couplings can also serve to reduce the intensity of shock load and vibrations transmitted from one shaft to another.

课文参考译文

第2单元 机械零件

机器在机械工业生产中起着重要作用。机械零件是组成机器的基本元素。本单元主要介绍常用的机械零件，如轴、轴附件、离合器、螺钉、弹簧、齿轮、联轴器、密封以及滚动接触轴承等。

2.1 轴

1. 实心轴

作为一个机械零件，轴通常是一个圆柱体的棒子，它支撑各种装置并随其转动，借以接收或者传递旋转运动及转矩。图2-1所示是一种典型的阶梯轴。

2. 柔性轴

与实心轴相比较，柔性轴可以弯曲至更小的半径而不会产生过应力。

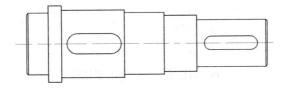

图2-1 阶梯轴

2.2 轴附件

键、花键和销的主要用途是阻止零件之间发生相对转动。

1. 键

键是置于轴和传递动力的轮毂之间的一个机械零件，用来传递转矩(见图2-2(a))。键是可拆卸的，便于轴系的组装和拆卸。键安装在一个轴上的轴向加工成的槽里，该槽称为键槽。在传递动力的轮毂上也有一个相似的槽，通常称为keyway，但更准确地说也称为键槽。键一般先安装到键槽里，轮毂键槽与键成一直线，轮毂滑到相应的位置。

直径6.5英寸以下的轴最常用的键类型是正方形键，如图2-2(b)所示。矩形键(见图2-2(c))适用于较大的轴和可以承受短边的较小轴。这两种键称为平键，因为它们的顶部、底部和各边都平行。

在轴和轮毂里设计键槽，键的一半高度是在轴的键槽里，另一半高度是在轮毂的键槽里。

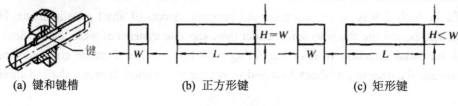

(a) 键和键槽　　　　(b) 正方形键　　　　(c) 矩形键

图 2-2　平键

2. 花键

花键是与轴做成一体的永久键,与轮毂里切出的键槽相配合。静配合和动配合尺寸都已标准化(见图 2-3)。

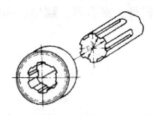

图 2-3　花键与连接

3. 销

圆锥销可以用于限制安装在轴上的元件作轴向运动和旋转运动(见图 2-4)。

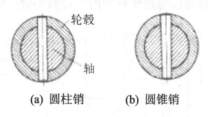

(a) 圆柱销　　　　(b) 圆锥销

图 2-4　用于传递转矩和定位的销

2.3　离合器

离合器是一种可快速方便地接合或分离一个转轴和另一个旋转着的同心轴的组件。离合器通常安装在机器的输入轴和驱动马达的输出轴之间,它提供了启动和停止机器的一种方便而快捷的方法,同时允许驱动马达或发动机在空载状态下启动。

机械离合器既可以提供无滑动的强制传动又可依靠摩擦传输转矩(见图 2-5)。

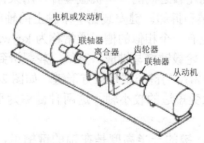

图 2-5　离合器的典型应用

2.4 螺钉

螺钉长期以来一直用作紧固件。螺钉由带有螺旋状凹槽的圆柱体或斜截头圆锥构成。带有螺钉起子槽的螺钉有几种形状的顶端，如平的、椭圆形的、圆形的。

带有六角形顶端的螺钉通常称为有头螺钉。这类螺钉用于当其中一个零件有内螺纹时把机器的零件夹紧在一起。如果零件上未切出螺纹，则必须使用螺栓。螺栓由带有六角形顶端的螺钉和螺母(是一个有内螺纹的六角环)组成，通常还有一个垫圈。

2.5 弹簧

弹簧是一个对载荷敏感、可储存能量的元件，其主要特性是允许大变形而不失效，且载荷撤销后能够恢复到初始尺寸和形状。

弹簧有多种用途，如在钟和手表里提供动力，对运输车辆减震，称重，进行弹性连接以及在装运过程中对精密器械提供抗震保护。弹簧和弹簧的应用如图2-6所示。

(a) 弹簧　　　　　　(b) 弹簧秤

图2-6　弹簧和弹簧的应用

2.6 齿轮

齿轮是有齿形的，圆柱形的轮子用来从一个旋转轴传递运动和动力到另一个旋转轴。主动轮与从动轮在空间啮合准确。主动轮齿推动从动轮齿运动，产生一个垂直于齿轮半径的作用力。因此，由于齿轮旋转，转矩和功率就被传递。

1. 直齿圆柱齿轮

应用最广泛的直齿圆柱齿轮齿形是全齿渐开线形式。它的形状特征如图2-7所示。

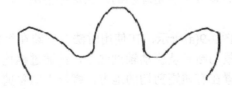

图2-7　渐开线齿形

渐开线是一种称为共轭曲线的几何曲线。当两个渐开线齿轮啮合旋转时，它们之间就会产生一个恒定的角速度。从初始接触的时刻到脱离啮合的时刻，主动轮与从动轮保持恒定的速度比例。两个齿轮产生的作用是很顺利的。否则在啮合时就会加速或者减慢，在系统中由此产生的加速度会造成振动噪声和危险的扭矩震荡。

渐开线曲线可以通过一个圆柱体和绕一根绳子在其圆周上来生成。在绳子的一端拴着一支铅笔。开始的时候铅笔紧紧靠着圆柱体，把绳子拉紧。移动铅笔远离圆柱体并保持绳子拉紧。这样画出来的曲线就是渐开线曲线。

通过这样一个圆柱体生成的圆我们称之为基圆。注意，在曲线上任意一点的位置，绳子代表基圆的切线，同时垂直于渐开线。在生成的渐开线与第一个基圆相切的位置沿着中心线画另一个基圆，这样可以看出，在接触点，两条线同时与基圆相切并将停留在同一位置与基圆一起旋转。

这发生在两齿轮啮合时。运动学(研究运动)的基本原理是，如果画出的线垂直于两旋转物体接触点的曲面，且总是在同一点横穿两物体中心线，那么两物体的角速度比值是恒定的。这是啮合的一种状态。正如所描述的，渐开线齿轮的齿形加工遵循这个原则。

2. 斜齿轮

斜齿轮和直齿轮的主要区别在于齿形的生成。在直齿轮中，齿形是直的并且与齿轮的轴线平行。在斜齿轮中，齿形与齿轮轴线倾斜一定的角度，这个角称为螺旋角。如果齿轮比较宽，它会显示出齿形以连续的、螺旋的路径绕着齿轮毛坯。然而，实际条件限制了齿轮宽度，因此轮齿往往仅仅显示倾斜于轴线。图 2-8 给出了两个通用的斜齿轮。斜齿轮的齿形与上述的直齿轮较接近。基本任务是用来说明螺旋角的影响。

图 2-8　斜齿轮

2.7　联轴器

联轴器是一种装置，它可以把两根轴的轴端连接起来借以传递动力。联轴器分为两类：刚性联轴器和柔性联轴器。

1. 刚性联轴器

刚性联轴器用来紧密连接两根轴，让两根轴之间不发生相对运动。这个设计对于一些需要或者提供精确直线度的装置来说是理想的。在这些情况下，联轴器用来在轴之间传递转矩。

典型的刚性联轴器如图 2-9(a)所示，在使用时法兰安装在每根轴的轴端并采用一些螺栓进行连接。然后传递负载的路径从驱动轴到法兰，再通过螺栓传递到连接法兰，最后输出给被驱动的轴。螺栓放置在有扭矩剪切的地方。螺栓上的总剪切扭矩取决于螺栓直径和扭矩。

刚性联轴器仅用于当两个轴不仅在机器安装时而且在机器工作期间对准并保持很精确。如果重要的角度、径向或轴向偏差产生时，在轴内部将会产生应力，应力是很难预测的且可能会由于疲劳导致早期失效，这些困难是可以通过使用弹性联轴器来克服的。

2. 柔性联轴器

当允许一些轴向、径向或角度偏斜时，我们可以用柔性联轴器来顺利传递扭矩，如图2-9(b)所示为一种柔性联轴器。柔性指的是当产生偏斜时，联轴器的部件可以进行微量调整。因此，在轴上没有明显的轴向或弯曲应力。市场上有许多种联轴器。每个联轴器用来传递指定的扭矩。制造商的目录里面列出了选用联轴器的设计数据。记住，扭矩等于功率除以转速。因此，对于一个给定尺寸的联轴器，随着转速增加，联轴器传递的功率也增加，但不总是成正比。当然，离心作用决定了转速的上限。

 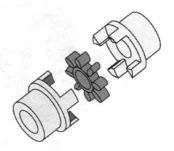

(a) 刚性联轴器　　　　　　　　(b) 柔性联轴器

图 2-9　联轴器

2.8　密封

在下列应用中，机械设计中的密封是十分重要的。
- 机器关键部位需要无尘。
- 在指定空间内必须要保持润滑。
- 带有压力的流体必须保持在元件内，如液压阀或液压缸。

某些参数会影响密封系统的选用、材料的使用和密封细节的设计，具体如下。
- 被保持或排除的流体的性质。
- 密封两侧的压力。
- 密封和配合部件的相对运动。
- 密封系统所有部件的温度。
- 密封需要的程度，是否允许少量泄漏。
- 密封系统的预期寿命。
- 密封用的固体材料特性：锈蚀性、平滑度、硬度、抗磨损性能。
- 磨损的密封元件容易更换。

密封系统的设计是无限的，在此只作一个简要介绍。通常，设计师依靠由密封系统或特定密封元件制造商提供的技术信息。同时，在关键或特殊情况下，建议对提出的设计做测试。

2.9　滚动接触轴承

轴承的作用是支承有相对运动的机器部件的负载。滚动接触轴承指的是在静止和移动部件之间采用了球状滚珠或者其他类型的滚珠的轴承，种类繁多。最常见的轴承支承一个旋转轴，承受纯径向载荷或径向、轴向载荷的混合。一些轴承仅仅用来传递轴向载荷。大多数轴承应用于旋转运动，也有一些应用于直线运动。

典型滚动接触轴承的部件包括内圈、外圈和滚动体。图 2-10 给出了常用的单列深沟球轴承。外圈常常是静止的，由机器的外壳支承。内圈压入到旋转轴且跟着一起旋转。滚动体在内外圈之间滚动。载荷路径从轴到内圈、滚动体、外圈，最后到达机器的支承上。采用滚珠允许轴顺利低摩擦地旋转运动。滚动轴承的摩擦系数大概在 0.001 到 0.005 之间，这些值只反映滚动元件本身和滚动体保留在轴承内的方式。

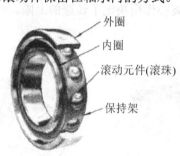

图 2-10 单列深沟球轴承

1. 滚动接触轴承的类型

在此我们讨论几种不同类型的滚动接触轴承及其典型应用。

径向载荷沿着轴承的径向方向作用在圆心上。这些载荷通常是由轴上传递动力的元件产生的，如直齿轮、V 带传动和链传动。轴向载荷是平行作用在轴线上的。斜齿轮、蜗轮蜗杆和锥齿轮上的轴向作用力都是轴向载荷。同时，由于轴的重量和轴上的元件也承受轴向作用力，支承垂直轴的轴承承受轴向载荷。偏斜是指轴在轴承上的中心线与轴承自身中心线的角度偏差。在图 2-1 中，优秀等级的轴承要求能承受高达 4°的角度偏差。一般等级的轴承可以承受 0.15°的偏斜，而较差等级则要求刚性轴的偏斜小于 0.05°。制造商目录应该有特定的数据被参考。

表 2-1 轴承类型的比较

轴承类型	径向承载能力	轴向承载能力	偏斜能力
单列深沟球轴承	良好	一般	一般
双列深沟球轴承	优秀	良好	一般
角接触球轴承	良好	优秀	较差
圆柱滚子轴承	优秀	较差	一般
球轴承	优秀	一般/良好	优秀
滚针轴承	优秀	较差	较差
圆锥滚子轴承	优秀	优秀	较差

2. 轴承材料

作用在滚动接触轴承上的载荷主要是作用在小的局部区域。无论哪种轴承类型，产生的接触应力都相当高。接触应力近 300 000 psi(注：psi 即磅/平方英寸，1MPa=145psi)的轴承在市场上并不少见。为了承受如此大的应力，滚珠、滚道和内外圈都需要用高硬度高强度的钢或陶瓷制造。

滚动元件和其他元件可以用陶瓷材料制造，如氮化硅。尽管花费比钢铁贵，但是陶瓷具有显著的优点。轻重量、高强度和耐高温的优点使得它们在航空、发动机、军事和其他需要的应用领域中得以应用。

Technical Reading

Machine Elements

In the manufacture industry, each machine is a combination of individual components generally referred to as machine elements or parts. Thus, if a machine is completely dismantled, a collection of simple parts remains, such as nuts, bolts, springs, gears, cams, and shafts—the building blocks of all machinery. A machine element is, therefore, a single unit designed to perform a specific function and capable of combining with other elements. Sometimes certain elements are associated in pairs, such as nuts and bolts or keys and shafts. In other instances, a group of elements is combined to form a subassembly, such as bearings, couplings, and clutches.

The most common example of a machine element is a gear, which, fundamentally, is a combination of the wheel and the lever to form a toothed wheel. The rotation of this gear on a hub or shaft drives other gears which may rotate faster or slower, depending upon the number of teeth on the basic wheels.

Other fundamental machine elements have evolved from wheels and levers. A wheel must have a shaft on which it may rotate. The wheel is fastened to the shaft with a key, and the shaft is joined to other shafts with couplings. The shaft must rest in bearings, and may be started by a clutch or stopped with a brake. It may be turned by a pulley with a belt or a chain connecting it to a pulley on a second shaft.

The supporting structure may be assembled with bolts or rivets or by welding. Proper application of these machine elements depends upon knowledge of the force on the structure and the strength of the materials employed.

Many machine elements are thoroughly standardized. Testing and practical experiences have established the most suitable dimensions for common structural and mechanical parts. Through standardization, uniformity of practice and resulting economies are obtained. Not all machine parts in use are standardized, however. In the automotive industry only fasteners, bearings, bushings, chains, and belts are standardized. Crankshafts and connecting rods are not standardized.

Unit 3 Engineering Materials and Their Properties

In industrial production, there are many types of engineering materials. Different engineering materials have different properties, therefore, engineering materials can meet the various needs of industrial production. The unit briefly introduces the types and properties of engineering materials.

3.1 Engineering Materials

All products that come out of industry consist of at least one and often many types of materials. The most obvious example is the automobile. A car contains a wide variety of materials ranging from glass to steel to rubber, plus numerous other metals and plastics.

The number of materials which are available to engineers in industry is almost infinite. The various compositions of steel alone run into the thousands. It has been said that there are more than 10,000 varieties of glass, and the number of plastics is equally great. In addition, several hundred new varieties of materials appear on the market each month. This means that individual engineers and technicians cannot hope to be familiar with all the properties of all types of materials in their numerous forms. All they can do is trying to learn some principles to guide them in the selection and processing of materials.

The properties of a material arise from the internal structure of that material. Just as the operation of a TV set depends on the components and circuits within that set. The internal structures of materials involve atoms, and the way atoms are associated with their neighbors into crystals, molecules, and microstructures.

In industry, engineers divide the materials into three main types: (1) metals, (2) plastics or polymers and (3) ceramics.

Characteristically, metals are opaque, ductile, and good conductors of heat and electricity. Plastics (or polymers), which usually contain light elements, and therefore have relatively low density, are generally insulators, and are flexible and formable at relatively low temperatures. Ceramics, which contain compounds of both metallic and nonmetallic elements, are, usually relatively resistant to severe mechanical, thermal, and chemical conditions.

Metals are divided into ferrous and non-ferrous metals. The former contain iron and the latter do not contain iron. Certain elements can improve the properties of steel and are therefore added to it. For example, chromium may be included to resist corrosion and tungsten to increase hardness. Aluminum, copper, alloys, bronze and brass are common non-ferrous metals.

Plastics and ceramics are non-metals; however, plastics may be machined like metals. Plastics are classified into two types that are thermoplastics and thermosets. Thermoplastics can be shaped and reshaped by heat and pressure, but thermosets cannot be reshaped because they undergo chemical changes as they harden. Ceramics are often employed by engineers when materials which can withstand high temperatures are needed.

3.2 Properties of Materials

While selecting a material, the primary concern of engineers is to match the material properties to the service requirements of the component. Knowing the conditions of load and environment under which the component must operate, engineers must then select an appropriate material, using tabulated test data as the primary guide. They must know what properties they want to consider, how these are determined, and what restrictions or limitations should be placed on their application.

Comparison of physical properties of the material is one means of distinguishing one material from another. These include such characteristics as density (weight); melting point; optical properties (such as transparency, opaqueness, or color); the thermal properties of specific heat, coefficient of thermal expansion, and thermal conductivity; electrical conductivity; and magnetic properties. In some cases, the physical properties may be of prime importance when one is selecting a material.

Mechanical properties are those responses a material has to the application of mechanical forces. Of specific interest are: (1) deformation (strain) which occurs when a stress is applied, (2) hardness, and (3) toughness. These mechanical properties are determined by subjecting prepared specimens to standard laboratory tests designed to evaluate the material's reaction to applied forces.

The properties of materials originate from their internal structures. If an engineer wants a specific set of properties, he must choose his materials appropriately so that they have suitable structures. Should the internal structure of a material be changed during processing of service, there are corresponding changes in properties.

A material's thermal properties become apparent when energy, which is introduced by the inflow of heat, causes the atoms to vibrate more vigorously and raises the temperature of the material. The results are: (1) thermal expansion, and (2) thermal conductivity.

Electrical properties are exhibited by materials which are subjected to applied electric fields. The more common electrical properties include: (1) electrical resistivity and conductivity, and (2) the relative dielectric constant, which relates the accumulated charge across an insulator to the electric field. These properties receive additional significance each year, since engineers must continually develop new and more automated products.

Words and Expressions

variety [və'raiəti]   变化，多样性

property	['prɔpəti]	属性，特性，性质
infinite	['infinit]	无穷，无尽，无限的
composition	[,kɔmpə'ziʃn]	组成，成分；作品
principle	['prinsəpl]	原理；原则；本质
originate	[ə'ridʒi,neit]	发起；发明；开始
internal	[in'tə:nəl]	内在的，本质的，固有的
analogous	[ə'næləgəs]	类似的，相似的
crystal	['kristl]	晶体，石英
molecule	['mɔlikju:l]	分子，微小颗粒
polymer	['pɔlimə]	聚合物
ceramic	[si'ræmik]	陶瓷
opaque	[əu'peik]	暗的，不透明的
ductile	['dʌktail]	有韧性的
conductor	[kən'dʌktə]	导体
insulator	['insju,leitə]	绝缘体
corrosion	[kə'rəuʒən]	腐蚀
tabulate	['tæbjuleit]	使……成平面，制成表格
transparency	[træns'pærənsi]	透明度，透明效果
opaqueness	[əu'peiknis]	不透明度
coefficient	[,kəui'fiʃənt]	系数；程度
conductivity	[,kɔndʌk'tiviti]	电导率，传导率
density	['densiti]	密度
deformation	[,di:fɔ:'meiʃən]	形变
strain	[strein]	应变
specimen	['spesimən]	样本，样品，案例
dielectric	[,daii'lektrik]	介电的，非传导性的，绝缘的
consist of		由……组成
range from…to		[范围]从……至……
run into		多达
associate with		与……相关
match … to		与……相配
the former…, the latter…		前者……，后者……

Notes

(1) A car contains a wide variety of materials ranging from glass to steel to rubber, plus numerous other metals and plastics.

句中短语 range from…to 是"[范围]从……至……"，plus 在此译为"加上，附加，另有"。

本句可以翻译为：生产一辆车需用大量不同的材料，包括玻璃、钢材、橡胶以及许多其他的金属和塑料。

(2) The internal structures of materials involve atoms, and the way atoms are associated with their neighbors into crystals, molecules, and microstructures.

associated with 在此译为"与……连接，与……有联系"。

本句可以翻译为：材料的内部结构包括原子，和原子之间相互连接形成的晶体，分子，和微观结构。

(3) These mechanical properties are determined by subjecting prepared specimens to standard laboratory tests designed to evaluate the material's reaction to applied forces.

by 在此表示"通过某种方式"，applied 在此是 apply 的过去分词形式，作为形容词。

本句可以翻译为：这些机械材料的性能通过把标本置于设计的标准实验条件下来测试受力时材料的反应。

Exercises

1. After reading the text above, summarize the main ideas in oral.

2. Comprehension questions.

(1) A car serves as an example because_____.
A. it used to be made of glass, then of steel and now is made of rubber
B. it is made of materials other than glass, steel and rubber
C. it is made of many materials including glass, steel and rubber
D. it is obviously made of plastics

(2) There are _____ varieties of glass and plastics.
A. hundreds of   B. more than 10,000
C. thousands of   D. more than 20,000

(3) Which of the following is not a material?
A. Metal   B. Rubber
C. Automobile   D. Glass

(4) There are about as many varieties of plastics as those of _____.
A. steel   B. glass
C. materials   D. rubber

(5) A material has certain properties because of its _____.
A. components   B. circuits
C. neighbors   D. internal structure

(6) According to the passage, materials are divided into three main types of _____.
A. ceramics, polymers or plastics, and metals
B. atoms, crystals or molecules, and microstructures
C. metals, plastics or ceramics, and polymers

D. internal structure, atoms or molecules, and metals

(7) Plastics are generally insulators because_____.

A. they are flexible and formable

B. their elements are of low density

C. they contain both metallic and nonmetallic elements

D. their internal structures involve atoms

(8) To make steel harder, _____ should be added to it.

A. aluminum   B. chromium

C. tungsten   D. ceramics

(9) The material resistant to high temperatures and corrosion is_____.

A. polymers   B. ceramics

C. metals   D. plastics

(10) Which of the following statements is true according to the text?

A. Copper, bronze, aluminum and brass do not contain iron.

B. The shape of thermoplastics can be changed by heat and pressure because of chemical changes.

C. When thermosets become hard, they can not be machined like metal.

D. Thermosets can withstand high temperatures when they harden.

(11) How many characteristics are mentioned in the passage as physical properties?

A. Five   B. Six

C. Seven   D. Eight

(12) Toughness, deformation and hardness are three specific _____ .

A. physical properties   B. mechanical properties

C. internal properties   D. thermal properties

3. Fill with the words given below in the blanks of the sentences from the text. Change the forms if necessary.

| number | resistant | compound | familiar | divide |
| component | originate | variety | numerous | associate |

(1) The properties of a material _____ from the internal structure of that material.

(2) A car contains materials of glass, steel and rubber, plus _____ other metals and plastics.

(3) Engineers cannot hope to be _____ with all the properties of all types of materials.

(4) It is convenient to _____ materials into three main types.

(5) The _____ of materials which are available to the engineer in industry is almost infinite.

(6) The internal structure of materials involves atoms, and the way atoms are _____

with their neighbors.

(7) Ceramics are usually relatively _____ to severe mechanical, thermal, and chemical conditions.

(8) A car contains a wide _____ of materials.

(9) Ceramics contain _____ of both metallic and nonmetallic elements.

(10) The operation of a TV set depends on the _____ and circuits within the set.

4. Translate the following phrases into Chinese according to the text.

(1) Engineering Materials
(2) range from…to
(3) run into
(4) associate with
(5) be subjected to
(6) consist of
(7) the former…, the latter…
(8) thermal properties

5. Translate the following phrases into English according to the text.

(1) 工程材料
(2) 材料性能
(3) 有韧性的
(4) 不透明的
(5) 电导率
(6) 从……至……
(7) 与……相关
(8) 与……相配

6. Write a 100-word summary according to the text.

课文参考译文

第3单元　工程材料及其性能

在工业生产中，工程材料的种类不计其数。不同的工程材料具有不同的性能，因此，工程材料能满足工业生产中的各种需求。本单元简要介绍了工程材料的种类及其性能。

3.1　工程材料

工业生产的一切产品至少由一种材料制成，经常是许多种材料制成的。最明显的例子便是汽车。生产一辆汽车需用大量不同的材料，包括玻璃、钢材、橡胶以及许多其他的金属和塑料。

在工业生产中，工程师使用的材料种类数不胜数。仅仅不同钢的合成种类就有成千上万。据说玻璃有一万多种，塑料的种类与玻璃的种类相当。另外，每月都有几百种新型材料上市。这就意味着不可能期望工程师和技师去熟悉各种材料的所有性能，他们所能做的只是去了解一些基本原理，以便在材料选择和加工时作为指导。

一种材料的性能来自其内部结构。这好比说，一台电视机的运行依赖于电视机内部的零件和电路。(材料的内部结构包括原子和原子之间的相互关联而形成的晶体、分子和微结构)。

工程师将材料分为三大类：①金属；②塑料或聚合物；③陶瓷。

金属的特点是不透明，有韧性，是热和电的良导体。塑料(聚合物)通常包含轻元素，因而密度较低，一般为绝缘体，并能在较低温度下弯折和成形。陶瓷是由金属和非金属元素的化合物构成，通常能抗恶劣的机械、温度和化学环境。

金属分为黑色金属和有色金属。前者含铁，后者不含铁。某些元素加进钢里能够改善钢的性能。例如：加铬后能耐腐蚀，加钨后可增加硬度。铝、铜、合金、青铜、黄铜等是常用的有色金属。

塑料和陶瓷是非金属。然而，塑料可像金属一样进行加工。塑料分成两类：热塑塑料和热固塑料。热塑塑料可通过加热和加压成形和再成形，而热固塑料却由于在硬化过程中发生了化学变化而不能再成形。工程师在需用耐高温材料时常常选用陶瓷。

3.2　材料的性能

在选用一种材料时，材料的性能与构件的工作要求是否匹配是工程师主要关心的问题。了解了构件必须运行的载荷条件和工作环境后，工程师必须以测试数据表为主要依据选用一种恰当的材料。此外，工程师还必须知道他们要考虑的是哪些性能，这些性能是如何测定的以及在实际应用中受到哪些约束或限制。

物理性能比较是一种区别材料的方法。这些物理性能包括：密度(重量)，熔点，光学性能(如：透性、不透性、颜色等)，特定热度、热膨胀系数和导热性等热性能，导电性和磁性。在有些情况下，物理性能可能是最重要的考虑因素。

机械性能指的是某种材料在施加机械载荷时所产生的反应。具体说就是：①施加一个应力时而产生的形变(应变)；②硬度；③韧性。要确定这些机械性能，就得使制备试样通过标准的实验测试，以测定材料在受力时产生的反应。

材料的性能由内部结构决定。如果工程师需要某些特定性能，他就必须正确地选用材料，确保这些材料具有适合的结构。如果材料的内部结构在加工过程中有了改变，其性能也就有相应的变化。

当热内流产生的能量引起原子较激烈的振动以及材料温度的上升，材料的热性能变得明显。其结果是：①热胀性，②热导性。

电性能是由施加电场的材料得以表现的。电性能通常有：①电阻率和电导率；②相对介电常数，即绝缘体的蓄电荷与电场的关系。这些电性能逐年得到越来越多的重视，由于工程师必须不断地开发新的和更自动化的产品。

Technical Reading

Material Substitution

As a new technology is developed or market pressure arises, it is not uncommon for a new material to be substituted in all existing design or manufacturing system. Usually, the result is improved quality or reduced cost, but it is possible to overlook certain requirements and to cause more harm than good.

Consider the drive to produce a lighter-weight, more-fuel-efficient automobile. The development of high-strength low-alloy steel sheets offered the ability to match the strength of many body panels with thinner-gauge material. As some of the original problems were overcome, the substitution appeared to be a natural one. However engineers must consider the total picture and be aware of possible compromise. Although strength was increased corrosion resistance and elastic stiffness were essentially unaltered. Thinner sheets would corrode in a shorter time and undesirable vibrations would be more of a problem. Design modifications would probably be necessary to accommodate the new materials.

Unit 4 The Design and Selection of Mechanism Systems

Mechanism systems play an important role in industrial production. Therefore, the reasonable design and selection of mechanism systems in industrial production is very important. This unit describes the design and selection of mechanism systems.

4.1 Design of Mechanism Systems

1. Mechanism Systems

According to system theory, a machine can be seen as a system of mechanisms and a mechanism is a sub-system of a machine. Hence, the design of a machine is the design of a mechanism system.

While some simple machines consist of only one kind of such mechanisms, in most cases, using only one simple mechanism is not enough to perform the required mechanical actions in a machine. Take the shaping machine as an example. Two working links (or output links) are needed to shape a flat surface. They are the sliding block with the shaping tool (cutter) and the worktable holding the workpiece. Carrying the cutter, the sliding block moves back and forth to perform the cutting motion and the stroke of this motion is adjustable to the size of the workpiece. The worktable moves intermittently to provide the feeding action while the sliding block moves back. The amount of feed is also adjustable. Such a working process needs several simple mechanisms working together to fulfill the whole function. These mechanisms operate together in a machine and form a mechanism system.

Another example of a mechanism system is the well-known internal combustion engine which consists of a crank and slider mechanism, two cam mechanisms and a gear mechanism, as shown in Fig.4-1. The crank and slider mechanism converts the back and forth movement of the piston into the rotation of the crankshaft. The gear mechanism and cam mechanisms control the movements of the valves exactly and ensure the synchronized operation of the whole engine.

The quality, performance and compatibility of a mechanical product depend mainly on its design. Any error, defect or carelessness in design may result in considerable extra cost in manufacture or even the failure of the product. The importance of design is obvious here.

2. Routine Design and Creative Design

There are different levels of design. When you design a machine useing similar models, you can design by imitation. Take one similar machine as a model, then, by keeping the main structure unchanged but changing some of the dimensions or sizes of the machine or replacing some parts with new ones, you can carry out the design quickly. Such a design is called routine design. If you design a totally new machine or apply a new working principle in a machine, you have to create a new structure, not just imitate the existing one. This is creative design. Of course, creative design is more difficult than routine design. Creative design plays an important part in developing new products to meet the growing demands of customers.

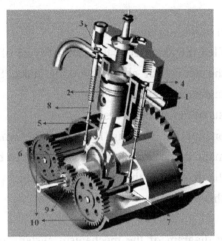

Fig. 4-1 A internal combustion engine

1—cylinder; 2—piston; 3—intake valve; 4—exhaust valve; 5—connecting rod;
6—crankshaft; 7—cam; 8—top rod; 9—pinion gear; 10—big gear

The kinematic function of a mechanism system is to convert the motion of a prime mover into the required motion of the output links of a mechanism system. To carry out the design of a mechanism system, an engineer should be familiar with the analysis, synthesis and design methods of various mechanisms. Furthermore, he or she should be able to choose the most suitable mechanisms and combine them into an integrated system. This requires some experience and technique about which various theories and methods are currently being developed.

3. The Design Process of a Mechanism System

Generally, the design process of a mechanism system can be divided into the following four phases:

(1) Planning of the product.

In this phase, the whole function of the product should be determined and the design task should be defined. Some investigation of the market and a feasibility analysis should be done here.

(2) Designing the kinematic diagram of the mechanism system.

This phase can be divided further into the following steps:

(a) Determination of the working principle of the machine.

Designers are required to have extensive knowledge of science and technology. Special attention should be paid to the so-called high technologies and their recent developments. Advanced working principles will produce excellent products if applied properly. Furthermore, the function of all working links should be prescribed.

(b) Type synthesis of the mechanism.

Suitable types of mechanisms should be chosen and combined into a mechanism system according to the technical requirements of the machine. The types of mechanism chosen should all perform the required motions. This is the most creative step, and effort should be concentrated on here.

(c) Drawing the diagram of the working cycle.

This diagram is also called the diagram of the motion cycle of the mechanism system. It is actually the timetable for the actions of all the working links. Such a diagram ensures the synchronization of all mechanisms in a machine.

(d) Dimensional synthesis of the mechanisms.

According to the actions of the working links and the working cycle diagram of the mechanism system, the kinematic dimension of the mechanisms can be determined.

(e) Drawing the kinematic diagram of the mechanism system.

This is the final step in this phase.

(3) Concrete design.

Based on the kinematic diagram of the mechanism system and the force analysis of the system, the structural design can be done. The technical drawing of all machine elements and the assembly drawing of the machine should be completed.

(4) Improvement of the design.

After a prototype machine is made, a series of tests should be carried out on it. Corrections can then be made to improve its performance. In the design process described above, some feedback or reiteration may be necessary to achieve a better result.

4.2　Selection of Mechanisms

According to the motion forms and kinematic parameters of working links and prime movers, mechanisms can be chosen to convert the motions of prime movers into those actions of the working links. One way to do this is decomposition and combination of the functions of the machine. Functions of the system are first resolved into several sub-functions or function elements. For each function element, all the possible function carriers (mechanisms which carry out the function) are listed. The combination of all the function carriers in each group provides a great many solutions among which some feasible ones can be chosen. Further evaluation of these feasible schemes will produce the best one.

Another effective way to select mechanisms is imitation and reformation. First, determine the key techniques of the machine to be designed and then search for the corresponding devices as models. According to the functions and design demands of the machine, the models can be reformed or combined and the mechanism system is determined. This method is often applied when relevant references can be found.

Unit 4 The Design and Selection of Mechanism Systems

It is now helpful to review different mechanisms with their kinematic functions.

1. Rotation Translating Mechanisms

These kinds of mechanisms are used to change the velocity and the direction of rotation. They can be divided further into three types.

1) Frictional mechanisms

This type of mechanism includes belt mechanisms (see Fig. 4-2) and frictional wheel drives. They are simple in construction and smooth in operation. Sliding in the mechanisms can provide protection against overload. They can be designed as stepless speed regulators. The drawbacks are the inaccuracy of transmission ratio, lower power capacity and lower efficiency.

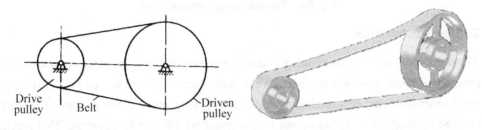

Fig. 4-2   Belt mechanisms

2) Engaging mechanisms

This type of mechanism includes gear mechanisms (see Fig. 4-3), worm gear mechanisms, chain mechanism, gear trains and so on. A chain mechanism is often used between two parallel shafts with longer center distances and lower accuracy compared to a gear mechanism. It operates less smoothly than gear mechanisms and should not be used at high speed. Gear mechanisms and worm gear mechanisms can transmit rotation between two shafts with any relative orientation. They have higher power capacity and efficiency and operate smoothly. They are used widely in a range of machinery.

Fig. 4-3   Gear mechanisms

3) Linkage mechanisms

Examples of this kind of mechanism are double-crank mechanisms, parallel-crank mechanisms and rotating guide-bar mechanisms, as shown in Fig. 4-4. Such mechanisms contain only lower pairs and provide various transmission functions. They are easy to be manufactured but not easy to be designed to suit the given transmission function.

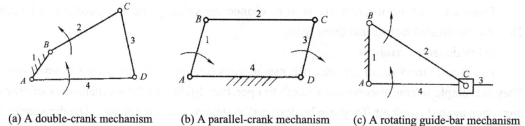

(a) A double-crank mechanism   (b) A parallel-crank mechanism   (c) A rotating guide-bar mechanism

Fig. 4-4   Typical linkage mechanisms

2. Step Mechanisms

The output link of a step mechanism can perform unidirectional motions with periodic dwells. The geneva mechanism, ratchet mechanism and index cam mechanism (see Fig. 4-5) are typical step mechanisms. A ratchet mechanism converts a rocking motion into a step (or intermittent) motion. The rotating angle of the output link (ratchet wheel) can be adjusted. This mechanism should be used only at low speeds and loads because of the impact between the ratchet wheel and the jaw. A geneva mechanism operates more smoothly than a ratchet mechanism, but the rotating angle of its output link cannot be adjusted. Index cam mechanisms are ideal step mechanisms for high speed application.

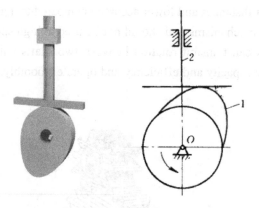

Fig. 4-5   Index cam mechanisms

3. Reciprocating and Rocking Motion Generating Mechanisms

Reciprocating and rocking motions are frequently used forms in machinery. Since rotation is the usual motion form of a prime mover, this type of mechanism should be used to convert a rotation into a reciprocating or rocking motion.

The slider-crank mechanism (see Fig. 4-6), crank and translating guide-bar mechanism and cam mechanism with a translating follower can convert rotation into reciprocating motion. The crank-rocker mechanism (see Fig. 4-7), oscillating guide-bar mechanism and cam mechanism with an oscillating follower convert rotation into rocking motion. Cam mechanisms can carry out almost any transmission function exactly with lower load capacity because of the higher pair. The lift of cam mechanisms is also limited within a small range to maintain a favorable pressure angle. On the contrary, linkage mechanisms cannot carry out exactly the given transmission function in most cases. But their load capacity and lifts of the output links are greater than those of cam mechanisms.

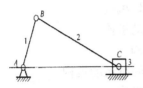

Fig. 4-6 Slider-crank mechanism   Fig. 4-7 Crank-rocker mechanism

Screw mechanisms convert rotation into translation with high accuracy and a great decrease in speed. It serves often as a fine tuning mechanism. It can produce great force with self-locking in the reverse direction. The efficiency of a traditional screw mechanism is not high, but nowadays, rolling mechanisms with high efficiency are available.

Similarly, the rack and pinion mechanism converts rotation into translation with a higher velocity, but it operates less smoothly than the screw mechanism.

4. Path-generating Mechanisms

Linkage mechanisms, geared linkages and some other combined mechanisms can serve as path-generating mechanisms. Four-bar linkages are the simplest ones and easy to be built. But they can generally follow the given path only approximately. Linkage mechanisms with more bars or geared linkages can sometimes do better, but still cannot follow the path exactly. Combined mechanisms with at least one cam produce almost any given path exactly but with higher cost due to cam manufacture.

Words and Expressions

piston	['pistən]	活塞
valve	[vælv]	阀门
compatibility	[kəmˌpætə'biliti]	互换性，通用性，一致性
prime mover	[praim]	原动机
imitation	[ˌimi'teiʃən]	模仿，效法
intermittently	[intə'mitəntli]	间歇地
feedback	['fi:dbæk]	反馈
mechanism system		机构系统
cam mechanism		凸轮机构
working link		执行件，传动件

gear mechanism	齿轮机构
sliding block	滑块
routine design	常规设计
shaping tool	成形刀具
creative design	创新设计
internal combustion engine	内燃机
the diagram of the working cycle	工作周期图
crank and slider mechanism	曲柄滑块机构
frictional mechanism	摩擦传动机构
ratchet mechanism	棘轮机构
index cam mechanism	凸轮式间歇运动机构
belt mechanism	带传动机构
frictional wheel drive	摩擦轮传动机构
crank and translating guide-bar mechanism	正弦机构
engaging mechanism	啮合传动机构
chain mechanism	链传动机构
crank-rocker mechanism	曲柄摇杆机构
linkage mechanism	连杆机构
oscillating guide-bar mechanism	摆动导杆机构
step mechanism	步进运动机构
geneva mechanism	槽轮机构
screw mechanism	螺旋机构

Notes

(1) While some simple machines consist of only one kind of such mechanisms, in most cases, using only one simple mechanism is not enough to perform the required mechanical actions in a machine.

while 在此表示"尽管，虽然"，在语气上有让步之意。

consist of 译为"包括，由……组成"。

in most cases 为状语，意思是"在大多数情况下，通常"。

本句可以翻译为：虽然一些简单的机器仅包括一种机构，但大多数情况下，在一台机器上仅用一个简单的机构并不足以完成所需的机械动作。

(2) Another example of a mechanism system is the well-known internal combustion engine which consists of a crank and slider mechanism, two cam mechanisms and a gear mechanism.

well-known 在此为"众所周知的，广为人知的"。

internal combustion engine 在此为"内燃机"。

本句可以翻译为：机构系统的另一个例子就是众所周知的内燃机，它包括一个曲柄滑块机构、两个凸轮机构和一个齿轮机构。

Unit 4　The Design and Selection of Mechanism Systems

(3) Any error, defect or carelessness in design may result in considerable extra cost in manufacture or even the failure of the product.

result in 在此为"导致，形成某种结果"。

considerable 在此译为"相当大的，相当多的"。

本句可以翻译为：在设计中的任何错误、缺陷或粗心大意都可能导致制造过程中大量的额外消耗，甚至是产品的失败。

(4) The slider-crank mechanism, crank and translating guide-bar mechanism and cam mechanism with a translating follower can convert rotation into reciprocating motion.

convert … into …在此为"把……转换成……"。

with a translating follower 在此为修饰语，修饰前面的"cam mechanism"。

本句可以翻译为：曲柄滑块机构、正弦机构和带有移动从动件的凸轮机构都可以将旋转运动转换为往复移动运动。

(5) Combined mechanisms with at least one cam produce almost any given path exactly but with higher cost due to cam manufacture.

Combined mechanisms 为"组合机构"，"Combined"在此为动词"combine"的过去分词形式，在此作为形容词，翻译为"组合的"。

due to 在此为"因为，由于"。

本句可以翻译为：至少带有一个凸轮的组合机构，几乎能精确遵循所给任何路径，但是由于凸轮制造导致成本较高。

Exercises

1. Answer the following questions.

(1) What is the routine design?

(2) What is the creative design?

(3) How many phases are there in the design process of the mechanism system? What are they?

(4) What is the most creative step in the four phases of the design process?

(5) Which kinds of mechanisms are introduced in this passage?

(6) How are mechanisms specified? Please describe the work process of mechanisms in your own words.

(7) How many kinds of mechanisms are used to change the velocity and the direction of rotation? Please describe the differences between them.

2. Translate the following sentences into Chinese.

(1) The worktable moves intermittently to provide the feeding action while the sliding block moves back.

(2) Take one similar machine as a model, then, by keeping the main structure unchanged but changing some of the dimensions or sizes of the machine or replacing some parts with new

ones, you can carry out design quickly.

(3) Suitable types of mechanisms should be chosen and combined into a mechanism system according to the technical requirements of the machine.

(4) Since rotation is the usual motion form of a prime mover, this type of mechanism should be used to convert a rotation into a reciprocating or rocking motion.

3. Translate the following phrases into English.

(1) 机构系统

(2) 凸轮机构

(3) 执行件，传动件

(4) 齿轮机构

(5) 内燃机

(6) 工作周期图

(7) 曲柄滑块机构

(8) 摩擦传动机构

(9) 棘轮机构

(10) 凸轮式间歇运动机构

4. Translate the following phrases into Chinese according to the text.

(1) belt mechanism

(2) slider-crank mechanism

(3) frictional wheel drive

(4) crank and translating guide-bar mechanism

(5) engaging mechanism

(6) cam mechanism

(7) chain mechanism

(8) crank-rocker mechanism

(9) linkage mechanism

(10) oscillating guide-bar mechanism

(11) reciprocating motion

(12) geneva mechanism

(13) screw mechanism

5. Write a 100-word summary according to the text.

课文参考译文

第4单元　机构系统的设计与选用

机构系统在工业生产中扮演了重要的角色。因此，合理地设计和选用机构系统在工业生产中显得尤为重要。本单元主要介绍了机构系统的设计和选用。

Unit 4 The Design and Selection of Mechanism Systems

4.1 机构系统的设计

1. 机构系统

根据系统理论，机器可看作是由多个机构组成的系统，而机构又是机器的子系统。因此，机器的设计就是机构系统的设计。

虽然一些简单的机器仅包括一种机构，但大多数情况下，在一台机器上仅用一个简单的机构并不足以完成所需的机械动作。以牛头刨床为例，加工平面需要两个执行件(或输出件)。它们是装有成形刀具(刨刀)的滑块和夹持工件的工作台。滑块带动刀具前后运动以实现切削，该运动的行程可根据工件尺寸来进行调整。当滑块向后运动时，工作台间歇移动以便提供进给运动。进给量也可以调整。这样一个工作过程需要几个简单的机构共同工作，才能实现全部的功能。这些机构在一台机器上共同运转就形成了一个机构系统。

机构系统的另一个例子就是众所周知的内燃机，它包括一个曲柄滑块机构、两个凸轮机构和一个齿轮机构，如图 4-1 所示。曲柄滑块机构将活塞的前后运动转换为曲柄轴的旋转运动。齿轮机构和凸轮机构准确地控制阀的运动，确保整个机器的同步运行。

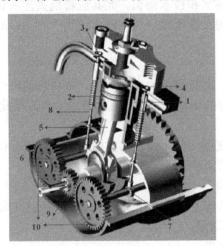

图 4-1　内燃机

1—气缸体；2—活塞；3—进气阀；4—排气阀；5—连杆；6—曲轴；
7—凸轮；8—顶杆；9—小齿轮；10—大齿轮

一个机械产品的质量、性能和互换性主要取决于设计。在设计中的任何错误、缺陷或粗心大意都可能导致制造过程中大量的额外消耗，甚至是产品的失败。由此可见设计有多重要。

2. 常规设计和创新设计

设计有不同的层次。如果采用类似的原型来设计机器，可以通过模仿来设计。取一个相似的机器作为模型，之后，保持主要结构不变，而改变机器的某些尺寸或大小，或者用新部件来替换其中的某些部件，这样就可以很快地完成设计。这样的设计称为常规设计。如果要设计一个全新的机器，或在机器中应用新的工作原理，就要创建一个新的结构，而不能仅仅模仿现有的。这就是创新设计。当然，创新设计要比常规设计难得多。在开发新产品以满足顾客逐渐增长的需求方面，创新设计起着很重要的作用。

机构系统的运动学上的功能就是将原动机的运动转换为机构系统输出件所需的运动。要完成一个机构系统的设计，工程师应该对各种机构的分析、合成和设计方法很熟悉。此外，还应该能够选择最合适的机构并将它们组合成为一个完整系统。这需要一些经验和技术(而这些技术，有着丰富的理论和方法)支持。

3. 机构系统的设计过程

一般说来，机构系统的设计过程可分为下列四个阶段。

(1) 产品策划。

在这一阶段，产品功能应该确定，设计任务应该明确。市场调查和可行性分析也应该完成。

(2) 机构系统运动图的设计。

这一阶段可进一步分为以下几步。

(a) 确定机器的工作原理。

设计者要拥有广泛的科学和技术知识。尤其应特别关注所谓高新技术和它们近来的发展。如果应用恰当，先进的工作原理可以生产出优秀的产品。此外，所有执行件的功能应该确定下来。

(b) 机构类型的综合。

根据机器的技术要求，选择合适的机构类型，并将它们组合成为一个机构系统。所选的机构类型都应能完成预定的运动。这是最具创新的一步，在此要集中精力。

(c) 画出工作循环图。

这个图也称为机构系统运动循环图。它实际上是所有执行件动作的时间表。这样一张图确保了机器中所有机构的同步。

(d) 机构的尺寸综合。

根据执行件的动作和机构系统的工作循环图，可以确定机构的运动尺寸。

(e) 画出机构系统的运动图。

这是这一阶段的最后一步。

(3) 具体设计。

以机构系统的运动图和系统的载荷分析为基础，可以完成结构设计。机器所有元件的技术图和机器的装配图也应完成。

(4) 设计改进。

样机完成后，应对它进行一系列的测试。接着就可进行修正以改进它的性能。在上述设计过程中，为获得更好的结果需要进行一些反复或反馈。

4.2 机构的选用

根据执行件和原动机的运动形式和运动参数，可以选择不同的机构以将原动机的运动转换为执行件的动作。做到这一点的一种方法是对机器的功能进行分解和综合。系统的功能首先被分解为几个子功能或功能元素。对每个功能元素列出所有可能的功能载体(即实现该功能的机构)。每一组中所有功能载体的集合提供了许多解决方案，选择其中一些可行的。对这些可行方案进一步评估，就可产生一个最好的方案。

选择机构的另一个有效途径是模仿和改进。首先，确定要设计的机器的关键技术，之后选择相应的装置作为模型。根据机器的功能和设计要求，可将模型改进或组合以确定机构系统。如能找到相关资料，常采用这种方法。

现在有必要介绍一下不同的机构以及它们的运动功能。

1. 回转运动传输机构

这类机构用于改变回转运动的速度和方向。它们可以进一步被划分为三种类型。

1) 摩擦传动机构

这一类型的机构包括带传动机构(见图 4-2)和摩擦轮传动机构。它们结构简单，运动平稳。机构中的滑动可提供过载保护。它们可被设计成无级变速的校准器。缺点是传动比不精确，传动功率和效率较低。

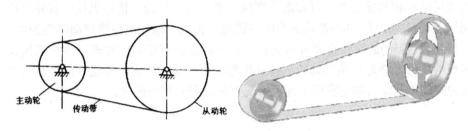

图 4-2 带传动机构

2) 啮合传动机构

这类机构包括齿轮机构(见图 4-3)、蜗轮机构、链传动机构、齿形链，等等。与齿轮机构相比，链传动机构常用在中心距较远的两平行轴间，并且传动精度稍低。它运转起来没有齿轮机构平稳，并且不能用于高速。齿轮机构和蜗轮机构能在任意相对运动方向的两传动轴间传递旋转运动。它们的传动功率和效率更高，运转平稳，被广泛应用于机械领域内。

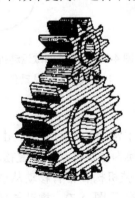

图 4-3 齿轮机构

3) 连杆机构

像双曲柄机构、平行双曲柄机构和转动导杆机构都是这种类型(见图 4-4)。这样的机构仅包含低副，提供不同的传递功能。它们易于制造，但要设计出满足给定的传递功能的机构却不容易。

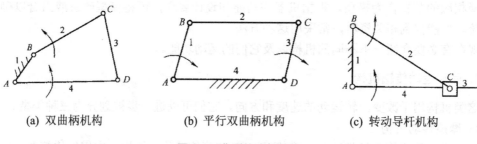

(a) 双曲柄机构　　　　(b) 平行双曲柄机构　　　　(c) 转动导杆机构

图 4-4　典型的连杆机构

2. 步进运动机构

步进运动机构的输出件，可实现周期性的单向间歇运动。槽轮机构、棘轮机构以及凸轮式间歇运动机构(见图 4-5)都是典型的步进运动机构。棘轮机构将摆动转换为步进(间歇)运动。输出件(棘轮)的旋转角度可以调整。由于棘轮和棘爪间的冲击，这种机构仅适用于低速轻载的场合。槽轮机构比棘轮机构操作起来更平稳，但它的输出件的旋转角度不能调整。凸轮式间歇运动机构是应用于高速情况下最理想的步进机构。

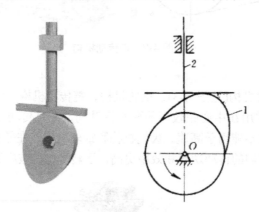

图 4-5　凸轮式间歇运动机构

1—凸轮；2—从动件

3. 往复移动和往复摆动机构

往复移动和往复摆动是机械中常用的运动形式。由于原动机通常是旋转运动，所以这种类型的机构用于将旋转运动转换为往复移动或往复摆动运动。

曲柄滑块机构(见图 4-6)、正弦机构和带有移动从动件的凸轮机构都可以将旋转运动转换为往复移动运动。曲柄摇杆机构(见图 4-7)、摆动导杆机构和带有摆动从动件的凸轮机构则将旋转运动转换为往复摆动运动。凸轮机构是高副，几乎能在低载下精确执行任意转换功能。凸轮机构的行程也限制在一个很小的范围内以保持一个适当的压力角。相反地，连杆机构在大多数情况下不能精确执行给定的转换功能，但是它们的承载能力和输出件的行程要比凸轮机构大得多。

螺旋机构将旋转运动转换为精度高且减速比大的平移。它常用作微调机构。它反向自锁时能产生很大的力。传统螺旋机构的效率并不高，但是现在的滚珠螺旋机构可达到很高的效率。

类似地，齿轮-齿条机构可以将旋转运动转换为更高速的平移运动，但运转时没有螺旋机构平稳。

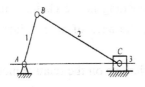

图 4-6　曲柄滑块机构

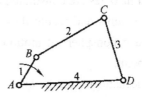

图 4-7　曲柄摇杆机构

4. 轨迹生成机构

连杆机构、齿轮连杆组合机构和某些其他的组合机构可用作轨迹生成机构。四杆机构是最简单的一种，制作也很容易。但它们通常仅能大致遵循给定路径。多杆机构和齿轮连杆组合机构有时做得更好，但仍旧不能精确遵循既定路径。至少带有一个凸轮的组合机构，几乎能精确遵循所给任何路径，但是由于凸轮制造导致成本较高。

Technical Reading

Mechanisms

Mechanisms may be categorized in several different ways to emphasize their similarities and differences. One such grouping divides mechanisms into planar, spherical, and spatial categories. All three groups have many things in common; the criterion which distinguishes the groups, however, is to be found in the characteristics of the motions of the links.

A planar mechanism is one in which all particles describe plane curves in space and all these curves lie in parallel planes; i. e. the loci of all points are plane curves parallel to a single common plane. This characteristic makes it possible to represent the locus of any chosen point of a planar mechanism in its true size and shape on a single drawing or figure. The motion transformation of any such mechanism is called coplanar. The plane four-bar linkage, the plate cam and follow, and the slider-crank mechanism are familiar examples of planar mechanism. The vast majority of mechanisms in use today are planar.

Planar mechanisms utilizing only lower pairs are called planar linkages; they may include only revolve and prismatic pairs. Although a planar pair might theoretically be included, this would impose no constraint and thus be equivalent to an opening in the kinematic chain. Planar motion also requires that axes of all prismatic pairs and all revolute axes be normal to the plane motion.

A spherical mechanism is one in which each link has some point which remains stationary as the linkage moves and in which the stationary points of all links lie at a common location; i. e. the locus of each point is a curve contained in a spherical surface, and the spherical surfaces defined by several arbitrarily chosen points are all concentric. The motions of all particles can therefore be completely described by their radial projections, or "shadows" on the surface of a sphere with properly chosen center.

Spherical linkages are constituted entirely of revolute pairs. A spheric pair would produce no additional constraints and would thus be equivalent to an opening in the chain, while all other lower pairs have nonspherical motion. In spheric linkages, the axes of all revolute pairs must intersect at a point.

Spatial mechanisms, on the other hand, include no restrictions on the relative motions of the particles. The motion transformation is not necessarily coplanar, nor must it be concentric. A spatial mechanism may have particles with loci of double curvature. Any linkage which contains a screw pair, for example, is a spatial mechanism, since the relative motion within a screw pair is helical.

Unit 5 Numerical Control

Numerical control plays an important role in manufacture field. The continually updated development of the numerical control(NC) technology promoted the development and progress of manufacturing. This unit mainly introduces numerical control principle, control system, computer numerical control and the advantages and disadvantages of numerical control.

5.1 Introduction

One of the most fundamental concepts in the area of advanced manufacturing technologies is (NC).

Controlling a machine tool using a punched tape or stored program is known as (NC). NC has been defined by the Electronic Industries Association (EIA) as "a system in which actions are controlled by the direct insertion of numerical data at some point. The system must automatically interpret at least some portion of this data". The numerical data required to produce a part is known as a part program.

A numerical control machine tool system contains a machine control unit (MCU) and the machine tool itself (see Fig. 5-1). The MCU is further divided into two elements: the data processing unit (DPU) and the control loops unit (CLU). The DPU processes the coded data from the tape or other media and passes information on the position of each axis, required direction of motion, feed rate, and auxiliary function control signals to the CLU. The CLU operates the drive mechanisms of the machine, receives feedback signals concerning the actual position and velocity of each of the axes, and signals of the completion of operation. The DPU sequentially reads the data. When each line has completed execution as noted by the CLU, another line of data is read.

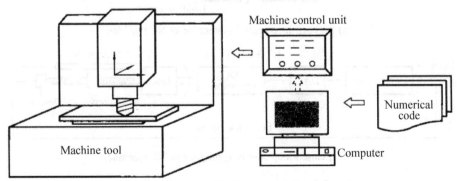

Fig. 5-1 A numerical control system

Geometric and kinematic data are typically fed from the DPU to the CLU and CLU then governs the physical system based on the data from the DPU.

Numerical control was developed to overcome the limitation of human operators, and it has done so. Numerical control machines are more accurate than manually operated machines, they can produce parts more uniformly, they are faster, and the long-run tooling costs are lower. The development of NC led to the development of several other innovations in manufacturing technology:

- Electric discharge machining.
- Laser-cutting.
- Electron beam welding.

Numerical control has also made machine tools more versatile than their manually operated predecessors. An NC machine tool can automatically produce a wide variety of parts, each involving an assortment of widely varied and complex machining processes. Numerical control has allowed manufacturers to undertake the production of products that would not have been feasible from an economic perspective using manually controlled led machine tools and processes.

5.2　Principles of NC Machines

An NC machine can be controlled through two types of circuits: open-loop and closed-loop. In the open-loop system (see Fig. 5-2(a)), the signals are sent to the servomotor by the controller, but the movements and final positions of the worktable are not checked for accuracy.

The closed-loop system (see Fig. 5-2(b)) is equipped with various transducers, sensors and counters that measure accurately the position of the worktable. Through feedback control, the position of the worktable is compared against the signal. Table movements terminate when the proper coordinates are reached. The closed-loop system is more complicated and more expensive than the open-loop system.

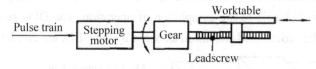

(a) An open-loop control system for an NC machine

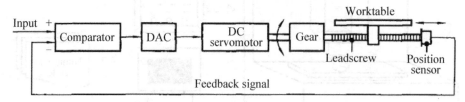

(b) A closed-loop control system for an NC machine

Fig. 5-2　Schematic illustration of NC machine

5.3　Types of Control Systems

There are two basic types of control systems in numerical control, point-to-point and contouring.

(1) In a point-to-point system, also called positioning, each axis of the machine is driven separately by leadscrews and, depending on the type of operation, at different velocities. The machine moves initially at maximum velocity in order to reduce nonproductive time, but decelerates as the tool approaches its numerically defined position. Thus, in an operation such as drilling (or punching a hole), the positioning and cutting take place sequentially.

After the hole is drilled or punched, the tool retracts upward and moves rapidly to another position, and the operation is repeated. The path followed from one position to another is important in only one respect. It must be chosen to minimize the time of travel, for better efficiency. Point-to-point systems are used mainly in drilling, punching, and straight milling operations.

(2) In a contouring system (also known as a continuous path system), the positioning and the operations are both performed along controlled paths but at different velocities. Because the tool acts as it travels along a prescribed path, accurate control and synchronization of velocities and movements are important. The contouring system is typically used on lathes, milling machines, grinders, welding machinery, and machining centers.

5.4　Computer Numerical Control

In the next step of the development of numerical control, the control hardware (mounted on the NC machine) was converted to local computer control by software. Two types of computerized systems were developed: direct numerical control and computer numerical control.

In direct numerical control (DNC), as originally conceived and developed in the 1960s, several machines are directly controlled, step by step, by a central mainframe computer. In this system, the operator has access to the central computer through a remote terminal. In this way, the handling of tapes and the need for a separate computer on each machine are eliminated. With DNC, the status of all machines in a manufacturing facility can be monitored and assessed from the central computer. However, DNC has a crucial disadvantage. If the computer shuts down, all the machines become inoperative.

A more recent definition of DNC (now meaning distributed numerical control) covers the use of a central computer serving as the control system over a number of individual computer numerical control machines having onboard microcomputers. This system provides large memory and computational capabilities and offers flexibility while overcoming the disadvantage of direct numerical control.

Computer numerical control is a system in which a control microcomputer is an integral part of a machine or a piece of equipment (onboard computer). The part program may be prepared remote site by the programmer, and it may incorporate information obtained from drafting software packages and from machining simulations, in order to ensure that the part program is bug free. The machine operator can, however, easily and manually program onboard computers. The operator can modify the programs directly, prepare programs for different parts, and store the programs.

Because of the availability of small computers having a large memory, microprocessor(s), and program-editing capabilities, CNC systems are widely used today. The availability of low-cost programmable controllers also played a major role in the successful implementation of CNC in manufacturing plants.

5.5 Advantages and Disadvantages of NC

Numerical control has given the manufacturing industry new and greater controls in the design and manufacturing of products. Today thousands of NC machines are in use in large and small machining shops. In these machining shops, NC may be used to control a simple drilling machine or to contour mill a part too complex to machine economically by conventional methods.

By using the NC, human error is greatly reduced. The NC machine produces accurate reproductions of engineering data and the consistency of parts is improved, resulting in less scrap.

NC machines can produce complex parts that could not be made by traditional methods or conventional machines.

NC reduces tools and fixture costs. Part of these savings is the result of the elimination of elaborate and specially designed tools and fixtures. Storage problems for tools and fixtures are also reduced.

NC increases flexibility. Engineering changes in production of parts are less costly and more rapid, since changes with NC are quickly accomplished by changing a tape rather than building new jigs and fixtures.

Production planning is easier and more effective with NC equipment because manufacturing capacity is more constant, predictable, and efficient. Cost estimates are improved because of the reliability and efficiency of NC.

NC reduces floor space requirements. Most NC machine tools can do many different machining operations on a part in one setup compared with traditional methods that include routing the part through several conventional machines. With a single NC machine capable of a variety of operations in a single setup, fewer fixtures are needed, smaller lots can be produced economically, and less storage space is needed.

NC machines require high initial investments. NC requires retraining existing personnel to become skilled programmers and operators.

Mechanical, electrical and electronic maintenance person are required when working with NC machines.

NC is not suitable to long-run application.

Words and Expressions

auxiliary [ɔːgˈziljəri]	辅助的，副的，备用的
synchronization [ˌsiŋkrənaiˈzeiʃən]	同时(性)，同步，周期
kinematic [ˌkiniˈmætik]	运动学的
tooling [ˈtuːliŋ]	给机床配备成套工具，工艺装备
mainframe [ˈmeinˌfreim]	主机，主计算机
discharge [disˈtʃɑːdʒ]	放电，卸下
assortment [əˈsɔːtmənt]	分类，分配，种类
transducer [trænsˈdjuːsə]	传感器，变换器
terminate [ˈtəːmineit]	使结束，限定
retract [riˈtrækt]	缩回，取消，撤销
terminal [ˈtəːminl]	终点站，终端
assess [əˈses]	评估，评定
versatility [ˌvəːsəˈtiliti]	多功能性，通用性
punch [pʌntʃ]	冲孔，打孔
flexibility [ˌfleksəˈbiliti]	柔性，灵活性
economically [ˌiːkəˈnɔmikəli]	经济地
maintenance [ˈmeintinəns]	维护
numerical control (NC)	数字控制，数值控制
human error	人工误差
result in	造成，导致
cost estimate	成本预测
floor space	工作空间
a single setup	一次装夹
storage space	存储空间
initial investment	初始投资
be suitable to	适合于
long-run application	长期应用

Notes

(1) NC has been defined by the Electronic Industries Association (EIA) as "a system in which actions are controlled by the direct insertion of numerical data at some point. The system must automatically interpret at least some portion of this data".

EIA 广泛代表了设计生产电子元件、部件、通信系统和设备的制造商以及工业界、政府和用户的利益，在提高美国制造商的竞争力方面起到了重要的作用。

本句引号中的前一句为 as 的宾语从句。

本句可以翻译为：美国电子工业协会对数字控制所下的定义为："一种各项工作都由在某个位置直接插入的数值数据来控制的系统。该系统必须至少能够自动解释这些数据的某一部分。"

(2) The CLU operates the drive mechanisms of the machine, receives feedback signals concerning the actual position and velocity of each of the axes, and signals of the completion of operation.

CLU 为本句的主语，后带三个动词作并列谓语。第二个分句中的 feed back signals 为动词宾语，concerning 引导的现在分词短语对其进行修饰。第三个分句中的 signal 为动词，表示"发出信号"，与前两个动词时态相同，构成并列谓语。

本句可以翻译为：CLU 操作机床的机械驱动装置，接收关于每个轴的实际位置和速度的反馈信号，并且发出控制信号完成操作。

(3) Numerical control has allowed manufacturers to undertake the production of products that would not have been feasible from an economic perspective using manually control led machine tools and processes.

that 引导的定语从句对名词短语 production of products 进行修饰。

From an economic perspective 的意思是"从经济的观点出发，从经济的角度来看"。

本句可以翻译为：数字控制使得制造商可以承担产品的加工，其产品的加工如果使用人工控制机床和加工过程，这从经济角度看是不太可行的。

(4) The path followed from one position to another is important in only one respect. It must be chosen to minimize the time of travel, for better efficiency.

respect 在本文中的含义为"方面，着眼点"。例如：

in one respect　　在一个方面，在一点上

in all respects (=in every respect)　　无论从哪方面(哪一点)来看，在各方面

in no respect　　无论在哪方面(哪一点)都不是……，完全不是……

本句可以翻译为：由一点到另一点的路径很重要，这只是一个方面。为了更高效，必须选择移动时间最短的路径。

(5) A more recent definition of DNC (now meaning distributed numerical control) covers the use of a central computer serving as the control system over a number of individual computer numerical control machines having onboard microcomputers.

serving as 为现在分词短语，作 a central computer 的定语。

having onboard microcomputers 为现在分词短语作定语，修饰前面的名词短语。

onboard 在文中的含义是"随车携带的，机载的"。

本句可以翻译为：DNC(现在表示分布式数字控制)的最新定义涵盖了"使用主计算机作为控制系统，来管理大量的带有机载微型计算机的独立的计算机数控机床"的含义。

(6) The part program may be prepared remote site by the programmer, and it may incorporate information obtained from drafting software packages and from machining simulations, in order to ensure that the part program is bug free.

part program 指的是"零件程序"。

remote site 意为"遥远的地方，远处"，在这里指"应事先编写好，不在现场"。

bug free 在这里的意思是"没有程序缺陷"。Bug 指"程序缺陷"，计算机系统或者程序中存在的任何一种破坏正常运转能力的问题或者缺陷。

本句可以翻译为：零件程序由程序员事先准备好，该程序应结合由绘图软件包和加工仿真中获得的信息，从而确保零件没有程序缺陷。

Exercises

1. After reading the text above, summarize the main ideas in oral.

2. Translate the following phrases into Chinese according to the text.

(1) the control loops unit (CLU)

(2) geometric and kinematic data

(3) the long-run tooling costs

(4) electric discharge machining

(5) point-to-point control system

(6) computer numerical control (CNC)

(7) synchronization of velocities and movements

3. Translate the following phrases into English according to the text.

(1) 数据处理单元

(2) 进给速率

(3) 轮廓控制系统

(4) 分布式数控

(5) 闭环系统

(6) 加工中心

(7) 零件程序

(8) 变换器、传感器和计数器

(9) 长期应用

(10) 人工误差

4. Fill in the blanks using the information given in the passage above.

(1) The advantages of NC are:

① _____

② _____

③ _____
④ _____
⑤ _____
⑥ _____

(2) The disadvantages of NC are:
① _____
② _____
③ _____

5. Translate the following sentences into Chinese.

(1) The CLU operates the drive mechanisms of the machine, receives feedback signals concerning the actual position and velocity of each of the axes, and signals of the completion of operation.

(2) The NC machine produces accurate reproductions of engineering data and the consistency of parts is improved, resulting in less scrap.

(3) Engineering changes in production of parts are less costly and more rapid, since changes with NC are quickly accomplished by changing a tape rather than building new jigs and fixtures.

(4) Most NC machine tools can do many different machining operations on a part in one setup compared with traditional methods that include routing the part through several conventional machines.

(5) Numerical control is a system of control that uses numerically coded instructions to operate motors and other devices that run a machine.

(6) Usually the machine function, such as a drilling operation, is also activated at each point by command from the NC program.

6. Write a 100-word summary according to the text.

课文参考译文

第 5 单元　数字控制

数字控制在加工制造领域具有举足轻重的地位。数控技术的不断发展，促进了加工制造业的不断发展与进步。本单元主要介绍数控原理、控制系统、计算机数字控制以及数字控制的优缺点。

5.1　简介

在先进制造技术领域里，数字控制是最基本的理念之一。

使用冲孔纸带或存储程序控制机床称为数字控制(简称数控，有时简写为 NC)。美国电子工业协会(EIA)对 NC 所下的定义为："一种各项工作都由在某个位置直接插入的数据来控制的系统。该系统必须至少能够自动解释该数据的某一部分。"用来加工一个零件的数据称之为零件程序。

数控机床系统包含机床控制单元(MCU)和机床本身(见图 5-1)。MCU 进一步划分为两部分：数据处理单元(DPU)和控制回路单元(CLU)。DPU 处理来自纸带或其他介质的代码数据，并传递每根轴的位置、需要的运动方向、进给速率及辅助功能控制信号到控制回路单元。CLU 操作机床的机械驱动装置，接收关于每个轴的实际位置和速度的反馈信号，并且发出控制信号完成操作。DPU 按顺序读取数据。当 CLU 执行完一行数据，则开始读取另一行数据。

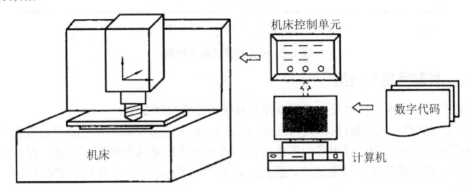

图 5-1 数控机床系统

几何和运动数据通常从 DPU 传给 CLU，然后 CLU 基于 DPU 的数据控制物理系统。

数控得以发展是用来克服人工操作的局限性，并且现在已经完成这项功能。数控机床比人工操作机床精度更高，它们能够加工一致性更好的零件，加工速度更快，且长期的工艺装备开销更低。数控的发展导致了加工技术领域其他几种新技术的发展：

- 电火花加工；
- 激光切削；
- 电子束焊接。

数字控制也使得数控机床比人工操作机床功能更多。数控机床能自动加工各种零件，每个包括了广泛的种类和复杂的加工过程。数字控制使得制造商可以承担产品的加工，而如果是使用人工控制机床和加工过程，这从经济角度讲是不太可行的。

5.2 数控机床的原理

数控机床通过两种回路控制：开环和闭环。在开环系统(见图 5-2(a))中，信号通过控制器传送给伺服电机，但工作台的运动和最终位置并未进行精确检测。

闭环系统(见图 5-2(b))带有各种精确检测工作台位置的传感器、检测元件及计数器。通过反馈控制，工作台的位置与该信号相比较。当达到合适的位置坐标，工作台停止运动。闭环系统比开环系统更复杂更昂贵。

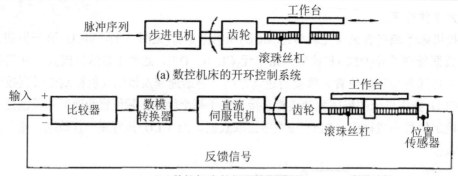

图 5-2 数控机床的图框说明

5.3 控制系统的类型

数控有两种基本控制系统：点到点控制系统和轮廓控制系统。

(1) 在点到点控制系统(也称为点位控制系统)，机床的每根轴由丝杠依靠操作类型，以不同速度单独驱动。为了减少非生产性时间，机床刚开始是以最快速度运动，但是当刀具接近它定义的位置时则会减慢速度。因此，在进行钻孔(或冲孔)操作时，定位和切削按照顺序执行。

孔被钻好或冲好后，刀具向上缩回并快速移动到另一位置，并重复操作。由一点到另一点的路径很重要，这只是一个方面。为了更高效，必须选择移动时间最短的路径。点到点控制系统主要用于钻孔、冲孔和铣削加工。

(2) 在轮廓控制系统(也称为连续路径系统)中，定位和操作都是沿着控制路径进行，但速度不同。由于刀具沿着指定路径运动，因此准确的控制、速度的同步以及运动都很重要。轮廓控制系统主要应用于车床、铣床、磨床、焊接机器和加工中心上。

5.4 计算机数字控制

在数控发展的下一步中，控制硬件(安装在数控机床上)通过软件转换为本地计算机控制。有两种计算机系统：直接数字控制和计算机数字控制。

在直接数字控制(DNC)中，正如 20 世纪 60 年代最初设想和发展的那样，几种机床通过中央主计算机一步一步地直接控制。在这个系统中，操作人员通过远程终端访问中央计算机。通过这种方式，处理纸带和每台机床上的独立计算机可以被取消。在 DNC 中，制造工厂的所有机床状态可以被中央计算机监测和评估。然而，DNC 有严重的缺陷。如果计算机停止工作，所有机床都无法运行。

DNC(现在表示分布式数字控制)的最新定义涵盖了"使用主计算机作为控制系统，来管理大量的带有机载微型计算机的独立的计算机数控机床"的含义。这个系统提供了大量的内存、计算能力和灵活性，同时还克服了直接数字控制的缺点。

计算机数字控制是一个系统，在该系统中控制微机是机床不可缺少的部件或装备(机载计算机)。零件程序由程序员事先准备好，该程序应结合由绘图软件包和加工仿真中获得的信息，从而确保零件程序无误。然而，机床操作者可以很容易地在机载计算机上编程。操作者能够直接修改程序，为不同零件准备程序，并存储程序。

由于小型计算机拥有大容量存储器、微处理器和编程能力，CNC 系统已被广泛应用。经济实惠的可编程控制器的使用对数字控制在制造工厂的成功应用起了重要作用。

5.5 数字控制的优缺点

数字控制给了制造工业新的和广泛的控制。如今，数千台数控机床应用在大大小小的加工车间里。在这些加工车间里，数控可用于控制简单的钻床或通过常规方法较经济地连续铣削一个复杂零件。

通过使用数控，人工误差大大降低。数控机床可精确根据工程数据重复加工，并且加工零件的一致性得到提高，废品率降低。

数控机床可以生产复杂零件，而这些复杂零件用传统方式或普通机床无法加工。

数字控制降低了刀具和夹具的成本。成本的降低部分是因为省去了复杂的和特制的刀具和夹具。刀具和夹具的存储问题也减少了。

数字控制增加了灵活性。生产中零件的工程设计变化只需较少的开支且更快，因为数控改变是通过改变纸带迅速完成，而不是通过制造新的夹具和配件。

因为数控设备加工能力更连续、可预测和高效，所以使用数控设备，生产计划更简单更高效。由于数控的可靠性和高效性，可以提高消耗的估算。

数字控制降低了工作空间需求。与传统的包括几台普通机床的工艺路线方式相比，数控机床在一个零件的一次装夹后可做许多不同的加工操作。对于一次装夹，可完成许多操作的一台数控机床，需要的夹具更少，可以经济地进行更小批量生产，而且需要的存储空间更小。

数控机床需要较高的初始投资。数控需把现有加工人员重新培训成为熟练的编程人员和操作工。

当数控机床工作时，需要配有机械、电气和电子维护人员。

数字控制不适于长期应用的情况。

Technical Reading

Numerical Control

Numerical control (NC) is a system of control that uses numerically coded instructions to operate motors and other devices that run a machine. The instructions are provided by either of the two binary coded decimal systems: the Electronic Industries Association (EIA) code, or the American Standard Code for Information Interchange (ASCII). ASCII-coded machine control units will not accept EIA coded instructions and vice versa. Increasingly, however, control units are being made to accept instructions in either code.

Numerical control instructions may be provided through a keyboard on a machine control unit (MCU), in the form of a punched tape, on magnetic tape, or directly from a computer. The current trend is to provide instructions directly from a computer.

Automatic operation by NC is readily adaptable to the operation of all metal working machines. Lathes, milling machines, drill presses, boring machines, grinding machines, tureet punches, flame or wire-cutting and welding machines, and even pipe benders are available with numerical controls.

There are two principal kinds of NC systems: (1) point-to-point and (2) contouring. Point-to-point control systems are simpler than contouring systems.

Point-to-point NC system is basically a positioning system. Its primary purpose is to move a tool or workpiece from one programmed point to another. Usually, the machine function, such as a drilling operation, is also activated at each point by command from the NC program. Point-to-point systems are suitable for hole-machining operations such as drilling, countersinking, counterboring, reaming, boring, and tapping. Hole-punching machines, spotwelding machines, and assembly machines also use point-to-point NC systems.

Contouring NC systems can direct the tool or work-piece to move at any angle, and also along curved paths. Many contouring NC machines, such as lathes and vertical milling machines are of the two-axis type. This type allows: continuous-path contours to be machined only in the XY plane. Three-axis machines are capable of simultaneous cutting movements in all three dimensional shapes in die and mold cavities.

Unit 6 NC Operation

With the more and more application of NC technology in manufacturing, NC machine tools play an irreplaceable role in machining, NC operation is very necessary. This unit introduces the knowledge of NC operation.

6.1 Describing the Operation Panel

Now the following Fig. 6-1 is a control panel of an NC machine tool.

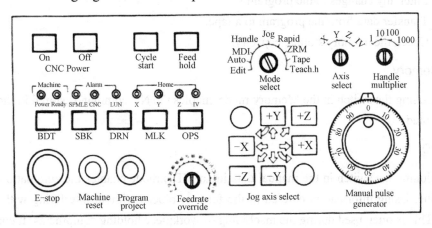

Fig. 6-1 A control panel

1. Emergency stop

The **Emergency stop (E-stop)** button is red and is located in the lower left corner of the control panel. If this button is pressed, the feed and rotation of the tool is stopped and the control system of the computer is turned off. The **Emergency stop** button is only used in special situations. Some of these are the overloading of the machine, a machined part is loose, or incorrect data in the program are causing a collision between the tool and the workpiece. To reset the **Emergency stop** button, push it in and turn it clockwise. Then you can turn the machine on, zero it, and eliminate the cause that forced the use of the **Emergency stop** button. Additionally, check whether any alarm signs appeared on the screen or whether the machine stopped during the execution of the cycle corresponding to a tool change or a table change. If such is the case, then repeat the same command (the cycle command) with the switch positioned on the MDI (manual data input) to make sure that the cycle has been completed.

2. Mode select

Use the switch (see Fig.6-2) to specify the operational mode. The position of this switch determines whether the machine utilizes the computer or the manual control.

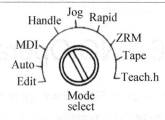

Fig.6-2   Mode select

3. Edit

Positioning the switch in the Edit mode enables you to:
- Enter the program to machine memory.
- Enter any changes to the program.
- Transfer data from the program to a tape.
- Check the memory storage capacity.

4. Memory

Positioning the switch in the Memory mode enables the NC commands stored in the memory to be executed.

5. MDI

Positioning the switch in the manual data input(MDI) mode enables the automatic control of the machine. Using information entered in the form of blocks without interfering with the basic program. This is often used during the machining of workpiece holding equipments. It corresponds to single moves (milling surfaces, drilling holes), descriptions of which need not be entered to memory storage. MDI can also be used during the execution of the program. For example, suppose you have omitted the command S350 M03 in the program. In order to correct this omission, turn on the SINGLE BLOCK switch and the position selector switch to the MDI mode. Using MDI, you can enter functions S350 and M03. Enter this command through Input and Start. The selector switch is positioned in the Memory mode to continue execution of the program from memory.

6. Handle

Positioning the switch (see Fig. 6-3) in the Handle mode allows for the manual control of the movements of the table with the use of the handwheel, along one of four axes: *X*, *Y*, *Z*, or *B*. By turning the handwheel clockwise, you can displace the tool in a positive direction with respect to the position of the coordinate system. By turning the handwheel counterclockwise, the tool is displaced in a negative direction with respect to the position of the coordinate system. The shaft of the handwheel contains 360 notches, each of which corresponds to 1° of rotation. Turning the handwheel, you can feel the displacement from one notch to the next. Handling the machine manually, use the additional speed switch (the handle multiplier), which can change the value of displacement equal to one skip on the scale of the handwheel. One full revolution of the handwheel (360°) corresponds to 100 units on the scale.

When the switch is positioned at

×1: turning the wheel by one unit corresponds to the displacement of 0.0001 in.

×10: turning the wheel by one unit corresponds to the displacement of 0.001 in.

×100: turning the wheel by one unit corresponds to the displacement of 0.01 in.

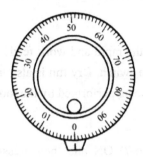

Fig. 6-3   Handle

7. Jog

Setting the selector switch in the JOG mode allows the selection of manual monotonous feeds along the X, Y, and Z axis. With the selector switch in the JOG mode, use the axis button (see Fig. 6-4), as well as the Jog feed rate (see Fig. 6-5) switch.

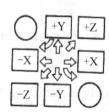 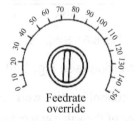

Fig. 6-4   Jog axis select   Fig. 6-5   Jog feed rate

8. Cycle start

Use this button during the execution of the program from MEMORY or TAPE. When the Cycle start button is pressed, the control lamp located above this button goes on.

9. Feed hold

When the Feed hold button is pressed, the control lamp located above the button goes on, and the control lamp located above the Cycle start button goes off. When the Feed hold button is pressed, all feeds are interrupted; however, the rotations are not affected. (This button is used very rarely.) During the execution of the threading cycle, Feed hold comes into effect after the tap is withdrawn. If the tap breaks during the threading cycle, the only way to stop the machine is by pressing the Emergency stop button.

10. Single block

The execution of a single block (see Fig. 6-6) of information is initiated by turning this switch ON. Each time the Cycle start button is pressed, only one block of information will be executed. This switch can also be used if you intend to check the performance of a new program on the machine or if the momentary interruption of a machine's work is necessary.

11. Dry run

By turning this switch ON, all the rapid and work feeds are changed to one chosen feed. In order to do this, use the Jog feed rate switch. Dry run is also used to check a new program on the machine without any work actually being performed by the tool.

12. Reference Return

Turning this switch (see Fig. 6-7) ON and then pressing buttons X, Y, or Z causes the machine to return to the zero position for each axis.

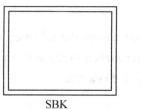
Fig. 6-6 Single block

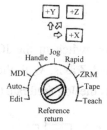
Fig. 6-7 Reference return

13. Feed rate override (see Fig. 6-8)

This allows the control of the work feeds defined by function F. You can increase or decrease the percentage of the value entered in the program.

14. Rapid traverse override

This switch reduces the rapid feed rate (G00). If it is positioned at 100, this corresponds to 100% of the feedrate that the machine can generate. Use this **Rapid traverse** button (see Fig. 6-9) to perform rapid movements along a previously chosen axis.

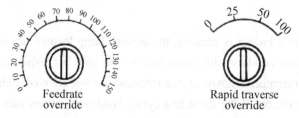
Fig. 6-8 Feed rate override   Fig. 6-9 Rapid traverse override

15. Machine lock

This switch is used to check a new program on the machine. All movements of the tool are blocked, while a check is ran on the computer screen.

16. Control panel

Usually, the control panel is located at the front of the main electronic system and is equipped with a screen and with various buttons and switches, as illustrated below (see Fig. 6-10).

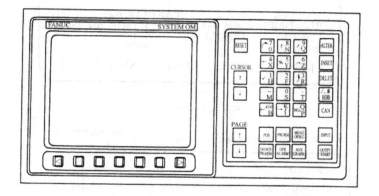

Fig. 6-10 Control panel (FANUC System)

17. Power on and power off

Notes:

(1) The control is always turned on after the main power switch, located on the door of the control system, is on.

(2) The control is always turned off before the main power switch is turned off.

18. Reset

Used for alarm cancellation or cancellation of an operation.

Attention:

The reset button should not be used while the machine is in working mode.

19. CRT character display

The screen on which all the characters (addresses) and data are shown (see Fig. 6-11).

20. Display

The contents of the currently active program are active sequence number displayed (see Fig. 6-12). In addition, scheduled next and the program list are displayed in the program:

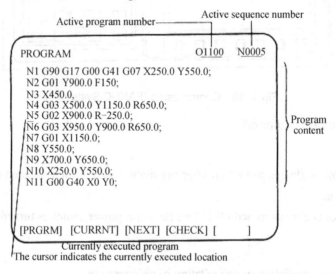

Fig. 6-11 Position

Fig. 6-12 Active program number

6.2 Screen Reading

Screen reading is an important skill that can be developed only through experience. This skill is especially needed when proving the program machining the first part. Many serious problems can be avoided through screen reading.

There are different screens on the monitor of a CNC machine. Some of them are presented below:

- Program screen.
- Position screen.
- Offset screen.

- Work zero screen.
- Parameter screen.

Each of these screens provides valuable information about the status of the machine tool. But the most important screens for the operator are the Offset screen and Position screen. If the machine has work shift capabilities, the work shift screen is also important for performing machine setup.

1. Offset screen

The lathe offset screens are similar for all lathes. Also, the machining center offset screens are similar for all machining centers. Following (Table 6-1) is the first page of the offset screen taken from one popular machining center.

Table 6-1 Tool offset

No.	Length		Radius	
	Geometry	Wear	Geometry	Wear
001	-19.1900	0.0000	0.0000	0.0000
002	-20.1300	-0.0100	0.0000	0.0000
003	-17.9000	0.0000	0.0000	0.0000
004	-20.7300	0.0000	0.0000	0.0000
005	19.8820	0.0000	0.0000	0.0000
...	...	...	...	...
015	-12.5770	0.0000	0.5000	0.5000
016	-10.2250	0.0000	0.3750	0.0000

In Table 6-1 the top is the name of the screen. The screen is divided into two parts: Length and Radius. These are short for tool length offset and tool geometry offset. The tool offset numbers are listed from 1 to 16. Geometry shows the offset entered when the setup was made, and wear shows the tool offset adjustment during machining.

The geometry offset number 002 has the value of -20.1300, and an incremental offset adjustment value of -0.01. Thus, the total value of this offset is -20.1310. Note that the geometry offset may also be adjusted in incremental mode. Then the wear offset would be zero. This means that if an offset adjustment is needed, it should be made in geometry or wear, but not in both (It is better to use wear).

Offset number 015 has a value of 0.5000 in Geometry offset and 0.0050 in Wear. This means that this program uses a 0.5-inch tool radius for geometry offset. The offset was adjusted for 0.005 inch during machining. Also, the adjustment can be made in geometry by entering 0.5050. Then the value in wear should be changed to zero. Again, better to use wear.

2. Position screen

The position screens are very similar for all of the controls. Following (Table 6-2) is the position screen taken from one popular type of lathe.

Table 6-2　Position

Relative	Absolute
U　0.0000	X　15.5720
W　0.0000	Z　5.0210
Machine	Distance to go
X　0.000	X 0.0000
Z　−749.300	Z 0.0000

　　The values in the Relative position express the relative tool distance from the home position. This distance is shown in the relative or incremental coordinates, U and W. When reading the values in the RELATIVE position, it is not possible to know directly how far the tool is from the part origin, just how far it is from the home position. The sign of the coordinates is zero or negative because the tool cannot move farther than the machine origin. Thus, at present, the values are zero, so the tool is at the home position. The values in the RELATIVE position are normally used when setting up the tools in order to find the real tool distances from the part origin.

　　The values in the Absolute position express the absolute tool distance from the part origin. This distance is shown in absolute coordinates, X and Z. The sign may be positive or negative, depending on the quadrants in which the tool is moving. This is an important piece of information for the operator when machining, since any value in the Absolute position is directly related to the part.

Words and Expressions

override　[,əuvə'raid]	超越，占优势
notch　[nɔtʃ]	凹槽，槽口
displacement　[dis'pleismənt]	位移量，偏移量
momentary	瞬时的
capability	能力，生产率
single block	单程序段
single operation	单步运行
reference return	基准复位
references datum(plane)	平面参考
threading cycle	加工螺纹循环
table feed	工作台进给
table longitudinal movement	工作台纵向移动
collision　[kə'liʒən]	碰撞，冲突
displace　[dis'pleis]	位移，偏移

tap	丝锥，抽头
cancellation	取消
MDI(manual data input)	人工数据输入
single execution	单步执行
dry run	空运行
references coordinate system	参考坐标系
reference system	参照系
sequence number	顺序号
table load	工作台承载

Notes

(1) If this button is pressed, the feed and rotation of the tool is stopped and the control system of the computer is turned off.

if 在此引导一个条件状语从句，表示"如果"。

本句可以翻译为：如果按下这个按钮，刀具进给和旋转将被停止，计算机的控制系统被关闭。

(2) Additionally, check whether any alarm signs appeared on the screen or whether the machine stopped during the execution of the cycle corresponding to a tool change or a table change.

additionally 在此表示"此外，另外"；whether 在此引导两个并列宾语从句。

本句可以翻译为：此外，在执行对应于换刀或工作台变位的循环中，检查屏幕上是否出现警戒信号或机床是否停止。

(3) Handing the machine manually, use the additional speed switch (the handle multiplier), which can change the value of displacement equal to one skip on the scale of the handwheel.

handing…为分词短语作时间状语，"which"引导非限定定语从句。

本句可以翻译为：在手动操作机床时，使用附加速度开关按钮(一种手动变换速度钮)，可改变手动轮转动一个刻度的位移量。

(4) This means that if an offset adjustment is needed, it should be made in geometry or wear, but not in both (It is better to use wear).

this means that… 在此表示"这意味着……"。

it is better to do sth. 在此表示"最好做某事"。

本句可以翻译为：这意味着，如果需要偏置调整，应在几何或 Wear 中调整而不要同时调整(最好用 Wear)。

Exercises

1. Interpretation of words and phrases.

(1) This is often used during the machining of workpiece *holding equipment*.

A. clamping device

B. secessions

C. chipper

D. plumbing

(2) During the execution of the threading cycle, FEED HOLD *comes into effect* after the tap is withdrawn.

A. comes into existence

B. comes into being

C. comes into action

D. comes into operation

(3) The execution of a single block of information *is initiated* by turning this switch on.

A. ceased

B. started

C. sponsored

D. pioneered

(4) This switch can also be used if you intend to check the performance of a new program on the machine or if the *momentary interruption* of a machine's work is necessary.

A. pause in a very short time

B. temporary trouble

C. arbitrary stop

D. pause for a long time

(5) Handling the machine manually, use the additional speed switch (the handle multiplier), which can change the *value of displacement* equal to one skip on the scale of the handwheel.

A. increment

B. position

C. movement

D. charge in position

2. Translate the following expressions into Chinese.

(1) manual data input

(2) single block

(3) single operation

(4) reference system

(5) table feed

(6) table longitudinal movement

3. Translate the following expressions into English.

(1) 单步执行

(2) 空运行

(3) 基准复位

(4) 顺序号

(5) 进给速率

(6) 控制面板

(7) 位移量

(8) 屏幕阅读

4. Decide whether the following statements are True (√) or False (×) according to the information of the text.

(1) The Emergency stop button is only used in the following situations: the overloading of the machine. (　)

(2) Reset button is usually used while the machine is in working mode. (　)

(3) The color of Emergency stop button is usually green. (　)

(4) To reset the **Emergency stop** button, push it in and turn it clockwise. (　)

(5) MDI can be used both to single moves (milling surfaces, drilling holes)and to the execution of the program. (　)

(6) By turning the handwheel clockwise, you can displace the tool in a positive direction with respect to the position of the coordinate system. (　)

(7) When the Feed hold button is pressed, all the movements of machine will be stopped. (　)

(8)When the Cycle start button is pressed, the control lamp located above this button goes on. (　)

5. Write a 100-word summary according to the text.

课文参考译文

第6单元　数控操作

随着数控技术越来越多地应用于机械加工中，数控机床在机械加工中起着不可替代的作用，数控操作就显得十分必要。本单元介绍了数控操作的一些知识。

6.1 操作面板的描述

图6-1是数控机床的一个控制面板。

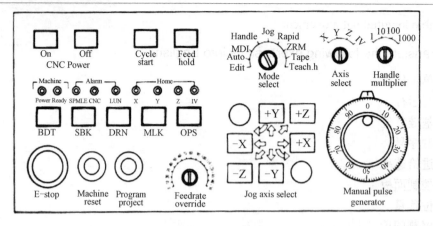

图 6-1 控制面板

1. 急停

"急停(E-stop)"按钮是红色的,位于控制面板的左下角。如果按下这个按钮,刀具进给和旋转将被停止,计算机的控制系统被关闭。"急停"按钮只在特殊情况下使用。这些特殊情况有机床过载、被加工的零件松动或者程序中的错误数据导致刀具与工件之间发生的碰撞等。要复位急停按钮时,可按下该按钮并顺时针方向旋转。然后就可以重新开机,按钮清零,排除被迫使用"急停"按钮的原因。此外,在执行对应于换刀或工作台变位的循环中,检查屏幕上是否出现警戒信号或机床是否停止。如果是这样的话,那么将开关定位在 MDI(人工数据输入)模式,重复同样的命令(循环命令)来确保循环能完成。

2. 模式选择

使用这个开关(见图 6-2)可确定操作模式。该开关位置决定机床是由计算机控制还是人工控制。

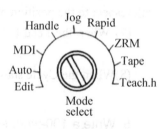

图 6-2 模式选择

3. 编辑

把开关定位在"编辑(Edit)"模式,你可以:
- 向机床内存输入程序。
- 对程序进行修改。
- 从程序向纸带传送数据。
- 检查内存容量。

4. 存储

把开关定位在"存储(Memory)"模式可执行存储在内存的 NC 命令。

5. MDI

把开关定位在 MDI 模式,可以利用与基本程序没有冲突的程序段形式进行信息输入,实现机床的自动控制。这种方法常用于工件支承装置的加工。它适应于单一运动(铣平面、钻孔),其描述信息不需输入到内存。在程序执行过程中也可以使用 MDI。例如,假如你在程序中漏掉了命令 S350 M03。为了纠正这个疏忽,打开"单程序段(SBK)"开关并把选择开关位置定在 MDI 模式。使用 MDI，便可输入指令 S350 和 M03，用输入(Input)和开始(Start)两个功能键输入这个命令，选择开关定位在"存储"模式，继续执行内存中的程序。

6. 手动

把开关(见图 6-3)定位在"手动"(Handle)模式，允许使用手轮沿着 X、Y、Z、B 四根轴中的一根轴对工作台的运动进行手动控制。顺时针旋转手动轮，可沿着相对于坐标系的正方向移动刀具。逆时针旋转手动轮，刀具沿着相对于坐标系的负方向移动。手动轮轴上有 360 个刻度，每一刻度对应于旋转 1°。旋转手动轮，你可以感觉到从一个刻度到下一个刻度的位移。人工操作机床，使用速度开关(手动倍率开关)能改变手动轮一个刻度的位移量。手动轮旋转一周(360°)对应于 100 刻度单元。

当倍率开关定位于

×1：按照 1 刻度单元转动手轮对应于 0.0001 英寸位移当量。

×10：按照 1 刻度单元转动手轮对应于 0.001 英寸位移当量。

×100：按照 1 刻度单元转动手轮对应于 0.01 英寸位移当量。

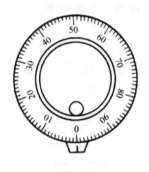

图 6-3 手轮

7. 点动进给

设置旋转开关在"点动进给"(Jog)模式，允许旋转沿着 X、Y、Z 轴点动单一进给。选择开关在点动进给模式时，使用轴选择按钮(见图 6-4)以及点动进给倍率开关(见图 6-5)。

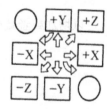

图 6-4 点动进给轴选择

图 6-5 点动进给倍率开关

8. 循环开始

在执行来自于内存或纸带的程序过程中可以使用这个按钮。当"循环开始"(Cycle start)按钮被按下时，位于按钮上方的控制灯亮。

9. 进给锁定

当"进给锁定"(Feed hold)按钮被按下时,按钮上方的控制灯亮,而位于"循环开始"按钮上方的控制灯灭。当"进给锁定"按钮被按下,所有的进给将被中止,但此时旋转运动不受影响(这个按钮很少被使用)。在执行攻丝循环时,丝锥被拉出后,进给锁定才开始起作用。如果丝锥在攻丝循环过程中折断,停下机床的唯一方法是按下急停按钮。

10. 单程序段

单程序段(见图 6-6)数据的执行是通过把这个开关置于 ON 开始的。每次"循环开始"按钮被按下,仅执行一个程序段数据。如果需要在机床上检查一个新程序的运行或者需要暂时中断一个加工作业时,也可使用这个开关。

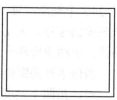

图 6-6 单程序段执行

11. 空运行

将这个开关(Dry run)打开,所有快进和工进都变成一个给定进给倍率。为了做到这样,使用"点动进给倍率"开关。"空运行"也用于在机床没有实际加工工件时检查一个新程序。

12. 零点返回

将这个开关(Reference return)(见图 6-7)打开,接着按下轴旋转按钮 X、Y 或 Z 会使机床返回每根轴的零参考点。

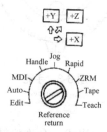

图 6-7 参考点返回

13. 进给倍率(见图 6-8)

这个按钮允许控制由功能指令 F 定义的工件进给速率。可以增加或者减少输入在程序里的数值的百分比。

图 6-8 进给倍率开关

14. 快速进给调节量

这个开关用来减少快速进给倍率(G00)。如果它被定位在 100，则对应于机床能发出的进给速率的 100%。使用"快速进给调节量"按钮(见图 6-9)可实现沿预先选定的轴快速移动。

图 6-9 快速进给倍率开关

15. 机床锁定

这个开关用于检查机床上的一个新程序。刀具的所有运动将被锁定，而程序在计算机屏幕上运行检查。

16. 控制面板

通常控制面板位于主要电子系统的前面，并配备一个屏幕及各种按钮开关和旋钮开关，如图 6-10 所示。

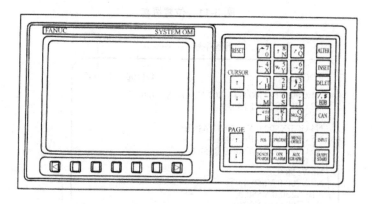

图 6-10 控制面板(Fanuc 系统)

17. 电源开关

说明：

(1) 数控系统总是在位于电气控制系统门上的主电源开关打开之后打开。

(2) 数控系统总是在位于电气控制系统门上的主电源开关关断之前关闭。

18. 复位

用于取消报警或取消某一项操作。

注意：当机床处于工作模式时不能使用复位按钮。

19. 屏幕特性显示

所有的特性(地址)和数据都可以显示在屏幕上(见图 6-11)。

20. 显示

当前运行程序的内容是以正在执行的顺序号来显示的(见图 6-12)。此外，程序还显示了下一个安排和程序表单。

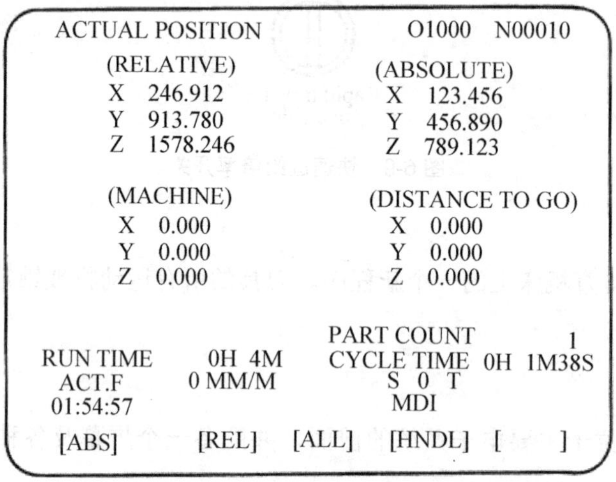

图 6-11 位置屏幕

图 6-12 当前运行的程序段号

6.2 屏幕阅读

屏幕阅读是一项重要技能，并且只有通过实践才能提高。当加工第一个零件验证程序时，特别需要这项技能。通过屏幕阅读可避免许多严重的问题。

在一台计算机数控机床的监视器上有不同的屏幕。下列为其中的几种。
- 编程屏幕。
- 位置屏幕。
- 刀具偏置屏幕。
- 工作零点屏幕。
- 参数屏幕。

每一个屏幕都提供了机床状况的许多有用信息。但对于操作者来说最重要的屏幕是刀具偏置屏幕和位置屏幕。如果机床具有加工模式转换能力,则对于执行机床设置,加工模式转换屏幕也是重要的。

1. 刀具偏置屏幕

所有车床上的刀具偏置屏幕都是相似的。而且所有加工中心上的刀具偏置屏幕也是相似的。表 6-1 中的内容是取自于一个常用的加工中心偏置屏幕的第一页。

表 6-1 刀具偏置

No.	Length		Radius	
	Geometry	Wear	Geometry	Wear
001	-19.1900	0.0000	0.0000	0.0000
002	-20.1300	-0.0100	0.0000	0.0000
003	-17.9000	0.0000	0.0000	0.0000
004	-20.7300	0.0000	0.0000	0.0000
005	19.8820	0.0000	0.0000	0.0000
...	...	...	...	...
015	-12.5770	0.0000	0.5000	0.5000
016	-10.2250	0.0000	0.3750	0.0000

顶端是屏幕的名称。屏幕被划分为两部分。

Length 和 Radius。它们是刀具长度偏置和刀具几何偏置的简写。刀具所列出的偏置号从 1 至 16。Geometry 表示刀偏设置时输入的偏置值,Wear 显示了在加工过程中的刀具偏置调整值。

刀具几何偏置号 002 的长度偏置值为-20.1300,增量偏移调整值为-0.01。偏置的整个值是-20.1310。注意到几何偏置也可以以增量方式调整。那么 Wear 偏置将是 0。这意味着,如果需要偏置调整,应在几何或 Wear 中调整而不要同时调整(最好用 Wear)。

偏置号 015 在半径偏置中偏置值为 0.5000,在 Wear 中偏置值是 0.0050。这意味着这个程序用 0.5 英寸刀具半径作为几何偏置。在加工中偏置被调整为 0.005 英寸。同时,调整也可在几何偏置中通过输入 0.5050 来完成。那么,在 Wear 中的值要改为零。而且,最好使用 Wear。

2. 坐标屏幕

所有控制器的坐标屏幕都很相似。下面(见表 6-2)是一台普通车床的坐标屏幕。

表 6-2 坐标位置

Relative	Absolute
U 0.0000	X 15.5720
W 0.0000	Z 5.0210
Machine	Distance to go
X 0.000	X 0.0000
Z -749.300	Z 0.0000

相对坐标位置中的值表示距机床原点的刀具相对距离。这个距离值用相对或增量坐标 U 和 W 表示。当以相对位置读取数据时，不可能直接知道刀具距离工件原点多远，只知道距离机床原点多远。坐标值符号是零或为负，因为刀具不可能比机床原点移动得更远。因此，当前值为零时，刀具正好在机床原点位置。相对坐标值一般在设置刀具时使用，以便于知道距离工件原点的真正刀具距离。

绝对坐标中的值表示刀具距离工件原点的绝对值。这个距离用绝对坐标 X 和 Z 表示。这个符号可以是正或负，具体要看刀具运动时在哪个象限。对操作者来说，加工时这是一个重要信息，因为绝对坐标中的任何值都是直接与工件相关的。

Technical Reading

Program Input and Output

1. Procedure for Inputting a Program

This section describes how to load a program into the CNC from a floppy or NC tape.

(1) Make sure the input device is ready for reading.

(2) Press the **EDIT** switch on the machine operator's panel.

(3) When using a floppy, search for the required file according to the procedure.

(4) Press function **PRGRM** key and display the program screen.

(5) After entering address **O**, specify a program number to be assigned to the program. When no program number is specified here, the program number used on the floppy or NC tape is assigned.

(6) Press soft key INPUT.

(7) To abandon the input at any point, press the RESET key.

2. Procedure for Outputting a Program

A program stored in the memory of the CNC unit is output to a floppy or NC tape.

(1) Make sure the output device is ready for output.

(2) To output a NC tape, specify the punch code system (ISO or EIA) using a parameter. To output the program to a floppy disk, select ISO.

(3) Press the **EDIT** switch on the machine operator's panel.

(4) Press function **PRGRM** key.

(5) Enter address **O** key.

(6) Enter a program number. If -9999 is entered, all programs stored in the memory are output. To output multiple programs by full MDI key at one time, enter a range as follows: O△△△△, O□□□□Programs No.△△△△ to No. □□□□ are output.

(7) Press soft key **OUTPUT/START**. The specified program or programs are output.

3. Explanations (Output to a floppy)

- File output location.
- When output is conducted to the floppy, the program is output as the new file after the files written from the beginning with making the old files in valid, use the above output operation after the No. head searching.
- An alarm while a program is put the floppy cassette is not specified as the input/output unit. Output with the soft keys when P/S alarm 86 occurs during program output, the floppy is restored to the condition before the output. The soft keys can be used to input a program. This operation is enabled if the floppy disk directory display function is not supported or, if the function is supported, the floppy cassette is not specified as the input/output unit.

Unit 7　Machine Tools

As the main processing equipment in the field of mechanical processing, machine tools have important influence on mechanical processing. This unit describes three kinds of commonly used machine tools, which are lathe, milling machine and machining center.

7.1　Lathes and Lathe Operations

Lathes are generally considered to be the oldest machine tools. Although woodworking lathes were originally developed during the period 1000 B.C., metalworking lathes with lead screws were not built until the late 1700s. The most common lathe (see Fig. 7-1) was originally called engine lathe because it was powered with overhead pulleys and belts from nearby engines. Today these lathes are setup with individual electric motors.

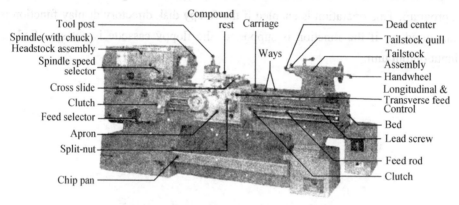

Fig. 7-1　Components of a typical lathe

1. Lathe components

Lathes are equipped with a variety of components and accessories. The basic components of a common lathe are described below.

1) Bed

The bed supports all major components of the lathe. Beds have a large mass and are rigidly built, usually from gray or nodular cast iron. The top portion of the bed has two ways, with various cross-sections, that are hardened and machined for wear resistance and dimensional accuracy during use.

2) Carriage

The carriage, or carriage assembly, slides along the ways and consists of an assembly of the cross-slide, tool post, and apron. The cutting tool is mounted on the tool post, usually with a compound rest that swivels for tool positioning and adjustment. The cross-slide moves radially in and out, controlling the radial position of the cutting tool in operations such as facing. The apron is equipped with mechanisms for both manual and mechanized movement of the carriage and the cross-slide by means of the lead screw.

3) Headstock

The headstock is fixed to the bed and is equipped with motors, pulleys, and V-belts that supply power to the spindle at various rotational speeds. The speeds can be set through manually-controlled selectors. Most headstocks are equipped with a set of gears, and some have various drives to provide a continuously variable speed range to the spindle. The headstock has a hollow spindle to which workholding devices, such as chucks and collets, are attached, and long bars or tubing can be fed through for various turning operations.

4) Tailstock

The tailstock, which can slide along the ways and be clamped at any position, supports the other end of the workpiece. It is equipped with a tailstock center that may be fixed (dead tailstock center) or may be free to rotate with the workpiece (live tailstock center). Drills and reamers can be mounted on the tailstock quill (a hollow cylindrical part with a tapered hole) to drill axial holes in the workpiece.

5) Feed rod and lead screw

The feed rod is powered by a set of gears from the headstock. It rotates during the operation of the lathe and provides movement to the carriage and the cross-slide by means of gears, a friction clutch, and a keyway along the length of the rod. Closing a split nut around the lead screw engages it with the carriage. It is also used for cutting threads accurately.

6) Workholding devices

Workholding devices are particularly important in machine tools and machining operations. In a lathe, one end of the workpiece is clamped to the spindle by a chuck, collet, face plate, or mandrel.

7) Accessories

Several devices are available as accessories and attachments for lathes. Among these devices are the following:

Carriage and cross-slide stop with various designs to stop the carriage at a predetermined distance along the bed. Devices for turning parts with various tapers or radii.

Milling, sawing, gear-cutting, and grinding attachments, and various attachments for boring, drilling, and thread cutting.

2. Lathe turning

In a typical turning, the workpiece is clamped by any workholding device described. Long and slender parts should be supported by a steady rest and follow rest placed on the bed, otherwise, the part will deflect under the cutting forces. These rests are usually equipped with three adjustable fingers or rollers, which support the workpiece while allowing it to rotate freely. Steady rests are clamped directly on the ways of the lathe, whereas follow rests are clamped on the carriage and travel with it. The cutting tool, attached to the tool post, which is driven by the lead screw, removes materials by traveling along the bed. The right-hand tool travels toward the headstock, and the left-hand tool toward the tailstock. Facing cutting are done by moving the tool radially with the cross-slide, and clamping the carriage for better dimensional accuracy.

7.2　Milling Machine and Milling

Milling includes a number of highly versatile machining operations capable of producing a variety of configurations (see Fig. 7-2) with the use of a milling cutter, a multitoothed cutter that produces a number of chips in one revolution.

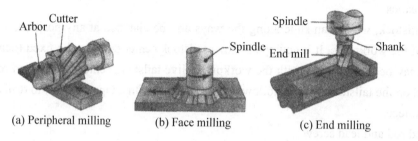

Fig. 7-2　Milling operations

1. Milling operations

1) Slab milling

In slab milling, also called peripheral milling, the axis of cutter rotation is parallel to the workpiece surface to be machined (see Fig. 7-2(a)). The cutter, generally made of high-speed steel, has a number of teeth along its circumference, each tooth acting like a single-point cutting tool called a plain mill.

2) Face milling

In face milling, the cutter is mounted on a spindle having an axis of rotation perpendicular to the workpiece surface (see Fig. 7-2(b)). Because of the relative motion between the cutting teeth and the workpiece, a face-milling cutter leaves feed marks on the machined surface similar to those left by turning operations. Note that surface roughness of the workpiece depends on insert corner geometry and feed per tooth.

3) End milling

Flat surfaces as well as various profiles can be produced by end milling. The cutter in end milling is shown in Fig. 7-2(c). It has either straight or tapered shanks for smaller and larger cutter sizes, respectively. The cutter usually rotates on an axis perpendicular to the workpiece, although it can be tilted to machine-tapered surfaces.

In conventional milling, also called up milling, the maximum chip thickness is at the end of the cut (see Fig. 7-3(a)). The advantages to conventional milling are: (a) tooth engagement is not a function of workpiece surface characteristics, and (b) contamination or scale on the surface does not affect tool life. This is the more common method of milling. The cutting process is smooth, provided that the cutter teeth are sharp. However, there may be a tendency for the tool to chatter and the workpiece has a tendency to be pulled upward, necessitating proper clamping.

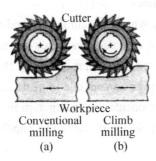

Fig. 7-3　Schematic illustration of conventional milling and climb milling

In climb milling, also called down milling, cutting starts at the surface of the workpiece, where the chip is at its thickest (see Fig. 7-3(b)). The advantage is that the downward component of the cutting forces holds the workpiece in place, particularly for slender parts. Because of the resulting high-impact forces when the teeth engage the workpiece, however, this operation must have a rigid setup, and backlash must be eliminated in the table feed mechanism. Climb milling is recommended, in general, for maximum cutter life in using computer numerical controlled (CNC) machine tools.

2. Types of milling machines

1) Column-and-knee type machines

Used for general-purpose milling, column-and-knee type machines are the most common milling machines. The spindle on which the milling cutter is mounted may be horizontal for slab milling, or vertical for face and end milling, boring, and drilling operations. The basic components of these machines are as follows:

A work table, on which the workpiece is clamped using T-slots. The table moves longitudinally relative to the saddle.

A saddle, which supports the table and moves in the transverse direction.

A knee, which supports the saddle and gives the table vertical movement so that the depth of cut can be adjusted.

An overarm in horizontal machines, which is adjustable to accommodate different arbor lengths.

A head, which contains the spindle and cutter holders. In vertical machines, the head may be fixed or it can be vertically adjustable, and it can be swiveled in a vertical plane on the column for cutting tapered surfaces.

2) Bed-type machines

In bed-type machines, the work table is mounted directly on the bed, which replaces the knee and can move only longitudinally. These milling machines are not as versatile as other types, but they have great stiffness and are used for high-production work. The spindles may be horizontal or vertical, and of duplex or triplex types—that is, with two or three spindles, respectively, for the simultaneous machining of two or three workpiece surfaces.

3) Other types of milling machines

Planer-type milling machines, which are similar to bed-type machines, are equipped with several heads and cutters to mill various surfaces. They are used for heavy workpieces and are more efficient than planers when used for similar purposes. Rotary-table machines are similar to vertical milling machines and are equipped with one or more heads for face-milling operations.

Various milling-machine components are being rapidly replaced by computer numerical control machines. These machine tools are versatile and capable of milling, drilling, boring, and tapping with repetitive accuracy.

7.3 Machining Center

Machining center has evolved from individual machines which, with the aid of man, performed individual processes to machines capable of performing many processes.

In 1968, an NC machine was marketed which could automatically change tools so that many different processes could be done on one machine. Such a machine became known as a "machining center"—a machine that can perform a variety of processes and change tools automatically while under programmable control.

The study of machining centers begins with the history of numerical control (NC). NC is programmable automation in which certain functions of the machine tools are controlled by coded instructions.

Computer and numerical control is used on a wide variety of machines. These range from single-spindle drilling machines, which often have only two-axis control, to machining centers, which can do drilling, boring, milling, tapping, and so forth with four-axis control. A machining center can automatically select and change as many as 32 preset tools. The table can move left/right or in/out and the spindle can move up/down or in/out, with positioning accuracy in the range of 0.0003 inch in 40 inches of travel. The machine has automatic tool change and automatic work transfer so that workpiece can be loaded/unloaded while the machining is in process.

The concept of automatic tool changing has been extended to CNC lathes. The tools are held on a rotating tool magazine and a gantry-type tool changer is used to change the tools. Each magazine holds one type of cutting tool. The versatility is being increased by combining both rotary-work and rotary-tool operations—turning and milling—in a single machine. Tools are changed in six seconds or less. It is common to provide two or more worktables, permitting workpiece to be set up while machining is done on the workpiece in the machine, with tables, being interchanged automatically. Consequently, the productivity of such machines can be very high, the chip-producing time often approaching 50% of the total.

Two new trends are observed in the development of machining centers. One is the growing interest in smaller, more compact machining centers and the other is the emphasis on extended-shift or even unmanned operations. Modern machining centers have contributed significantly to improved productivity in many companies. They have eliminated the time lost in moving workpieces from machine to machine and the time needed for workpiece loading and unloading for separate operations. In addition, they have minimized the time lost in changing tools, carrying out gauging operations, and aligning workpieces on the machine.

Words and Expressions

lathe	[leið]	车床
carriage	['kæridʒ]	(车床的)拖板，机床的滑动台架
arbor	['ɑ:bə]	支持切割刀具的条棒；刀轴
apron	['eiprən]	挡板，溜板
collet	['kɔlit]	筒夹，夹头
necessitate	[ni'sesi‚teit]	成为必要
contamination	[kən‚tæmi'neiʃən]	污染，污染物
cross-slide		横向拖板
lead screw		丝杠
face milling		平面铣法，阔面铣削
down milling		顺铣，同向铣切
accessory	[æk'sesəri]	附件
chuck	[tʃʌk]	卡盘，夹盘
mandrel	['mændrəl]	心轴
circumference	[sə'kʌmfərəns]	圆周，周围
cast iron		铸铁
feed rod		光杆，分配杆，进给杆
up milling		仰铣，对向铣，逆铣
depth of cut		切削深度

Notes

(1) The apron is equipped with mechanisms for both manual and mechanized movement of the carriage and the cross-slide by means of the lead screw.

be equipped with：装(配)备，安装；来自于 equip sth. with(用……装备，使装(具)备)的被动语态。by means of：依靠，通过……手段。

本句可以翻译为：溜板箱上安装有一些机械装置，通过丝杠来实现刀架(或托板)和横托板的手动或机械的运动。

(2) It rotates during the operation of the lathe and provides movement to the carriage and the cross-slide by means of gears, a friction clutch, and a keyway along the length of the rod. Closing a split nut around the lead screw engages it with the carriage. It is also used for cutting

threads accurately.

第一句是一个并列句，It 为主语，根据上文可知它指光杠，后接并列谓语 rotates 和 provides 及各自的宾语部分。

第二句中动名词短语 Closing a split nut around the lead screw 作主语，engages 为其谓语部分，it 指丝杠；engage with 意指"与……啮合，搭合"。

这几句可以翻译为：它(光杠)在车床的操作过程中旋转，并通过齿轮、摩擦离合器和沿着光杠长度方向上的键槽的配合为刀架(或托板)和横托板提供运动。将一个劈开的螺母与丝杠啮合，就使得丝杠与刀架(或托板)啮合。这同样被用于螺纹的精确加工。

(3) Because of the resulting high-impact forces when the teeth engage the workpiece, however, this operation must have a rigid setup, and backlash must be eliminated in the table feed mechanism.

high-impact forces 在此译为"高冲击力"。

本句可以翻译为：然而，由于当齿轮与工件啮合时导致的高冲击力，此操作必须要有一个刚性的安装支撑，并且必须消除工作台进给机构的后冲。

(4) The spindle on which the milling cutter is mounted may be horizontal for slab milling, or vertical for face and end milling, boring, and drilling operations.

slab milling 指的是"周铣"。

face milling 指的是"平面铣削"。

end milling 指的是"端铣"。

此句可以翻译为：在周铣中，铣刀安装轴是水平安装的，而在平面铣削和端铣、镗削和钻孔加工中铣刀安装轴是垂直安装的。

(5) Because of the relative motion between the cutting teeth and the workpiece, a face-milling cutter leaves feed marks on the machined surface similar to those left by turning operations.

在此，face-milling 指的"是端(面)铣(削)"，turning 指的是"车削"。

本句可以翻译为：由于切削刀齿和工件之间的相对运动，平(面)铣(削)刀具在加工表面上留下的进给痕迹类似于车削加工留下的痕迹。

Exercises

1. After reading the text above, summarize the main ideas in oral.

2. Fill in the blanks with proper words or phrases according to the text (note the proper tense).

(1) The most common lathe was originally called e____ because it was powered with overhead p____ and b____ from nearby engines.

(2) Lathes are equipped with a variety of components and accessories. The basic components of a common lathe are b____, c____, h____, t____, f____, w____, and a____.

(3) Steady rests are clamped directly o____ of the lathe, whereas follow rests are clamped o____ and travel with it.

(4) According to the direction that the cutter fed to the workpiece, the milling action can be divided into u____ and d____.

(5) Milling operations include p____, f____ and e____.

(6) The basic components of milling machines are included w____, s____, k____, o____ and h____.

3. Comprehension questions.

(1) A machining center is _____.
A. a machine that is capable of performing many processes
B. a machine that performs many processes at the same time
C. a center that automatically controls many machines
D. a wide variety of machines under programmable control

(2) The machining center can automatically select and change the tools that _____.
A. move left and right
B. have been preset
C. move up and down
D. are loaded and unloaded

(3) A single NC machine is the same as a machining center in the fact that _____.
A. both of them can select and change tools
B. both of them must be programmed
C. both of them use a tool magazine
D. both of them have two or more worktables

(4) The machining center is built to _____ productivity by _____ the time for changing tools, gauging operations and aligning workpieces.
A. approach … minimizing
B. minimize … eliminating
C. improve … eliminating
D. increase … reducing

(5) According to the current trends, machining centers will be made _____.
A. smaller in size and more automatic in operations
B. capable of performing in less time and for higher productivity
C. more compact and for more emphases
D. for more companies and higher productivity

4. Translate the following phrases into Chinese according to the text.

(1) engine lathe
(2) compound rest
(3) wear resistance and dimensional accuracy
(4) an axis perpendicular to the workpiece
(5) face milling

(6) column-and-knee type machines

(7) boring and drilling operations

(8) be mounted on the tailstock quill

5. Translate the following phrases into English according to the text.

(1) 主轴

(2) 溜板箱

(3) 托板

(4) 周铣

(5) 光杠和丝杠

(6) 高冲击力

(7) 螺纹切削加工

6. Translate the following sentence into Chinese.

(1) The most common lathe was originally called engine lathe because it was powered with overhead pulleys and belts from nearby engines.

(2) The top portion of the bed has two ways, with various cross-sections, that are hardened and machined for wear resistance and dimensional accuracy during use.

(3) The advantage is that the downward component of the cutting forces holds the workpiece in place, particularly for slender parts.

(4) The spindle on which the milling cutter is mounted may be horizontal for slab milling, or vertical for face and end milling, boring, and drilling operations.

(5) In vertical machines, the head may be fixed or it can be vertically adjustable, and it can be swiveled in a vertical plane on the column for cutting tapered surfaces.

7. Write a 100-word summary according to the text.

课文参考译文

第7单元 机床

机床作为机械加工领域中主要的加工设备，对机械加工有着重要的影响。本单元介绍了三种常用的机床：车床、铣床和加工中心。

7.1 车床及车削加工

车床被认为是最古老的机床。尽管木材加工车床早在公元前 1000 年就出现了，但直到 18 世纪晚期带有丝杠的金属切削车床才出现。最常见的车床(见图 7-1)称为机力车床，由于它是由旁边的发动机通过悬挂皮带轮及皮带传递动力。目前，这些车床都各自带有电动机。

1. 车床部件

车床配有大量的部件和附件。普通车床的基本部件描述如下。

1) 床身

床身支承了车床上的所有主要部件。床身具有大的重量并采用灰铸铁和球墨铸铁刚性制造而成。床身的顶部具有两条导轨,导轨的横截面形式多种多样,为了提高使用时的耐磨性和尺寸精度,对导轨进行了强化和加工处理。

2) 车床拖板

车床拖板或车床附件沿着导轨滑动,它是由横向拖板、刀架、溜板装配而成的。切削刀具安装在刀架上,通常带有一个复合中心架便于刀具旋转定位和调整。横向拖板沿着径向移动,在端面车削等操作中控制刀具的径向位置。溜板箱上安装有一些机械装置,通过丝杠来实现刀架(或拖板)和横向拖板的手动或机械的运动。

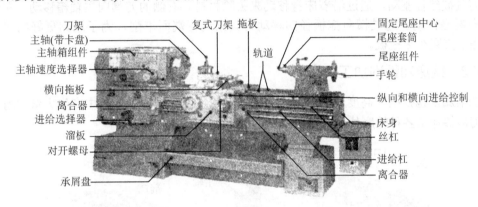

图 7-1 典型车床的零部件组成图

3) 主轴箱

主轴箱固定在床身上,并配有电动机、带轮和 V 带,它们可向主轴提供不同的转速。通过手动控制选择器能设定主轴的转速。大多数主轴箱配有一套齿轮,还有一些主轴箱具有多种驱动方式,可以向主轴提供连续变化的速度。主轴箱有一个中空的主轴,和夹紧装置(如卡盘、夹头)是连在一起的,且长棒和管类工件可进行多种切削操作进给。

4) 尾座

尾座可沿着导轨滑动,并可以在任意位置被夹紧,它支承工件的另一端。尾座上装有一个尾座中心,它可能是固定的(固定尾座中心)或随工件自由转动的(活动尾座中心)。钻头和铰刀能安装在尾座套筒上(一个带有锥度的中空的圆柱体零件)来钻工件的轴向孔。

5) 光杠和丝杠

光杠是由主轴箱的一套齿轮提供动力。它(光杠)在车床的操作过程中旋转,并通过齿轮、摩擦离合器和沿着光杠长度方向上的键槽的配合为刀架(或托板)和横托板提供运动。将一个劈开的螺母与丝杠啮合,就使得丝杠与刀架(或拖板)啮合。这同样被用于螺纹的精确加工。

6) 夹紧装置

夹紧装置在机床及机床加工中是十分重要的。在车床加工中,工件的一端被卡盘、夹头、花盘或心轴夹紧到主轴上。

7) 附件

有几种装置是车床上的附件和附属部件。这些装置如下。

车床拖板和带有各种设计的横向拖板停止器，用来让拖板停在沿着床身预先设定的位移。带有各种锥度和半径的车削零件的装置。

铣、锯、切齿和磨削附件，以及各种镗、钻和螺纹切削附件。

2．车床车削加工

在一般的车削加工中，工件可被前述的任意夹紧装置夹紧。细长的工件应该用床身上的固定中心架和移动中心架来支承，否则，在切削力的作用下零件会发生变形。这些中心架常带有三个可调节的爪子或滚筒，当允许工件自由旋转时，它们可用来支承工件。固定中心架被直接夹紧在车床的导轨上，而移动中心架被夹紧在拖板上并随之移动。装在刀架上的刀具被丝杠驱动，通过沿着床身移动来去除材料。右侧的刀具向主轴箱移动，左侧的刀具向尾座移动。通过横向拖板径向移动刀具来进行端面车削，为了达到更好的尺寸精度，需要夹紧车床拖板。

7.2 铣床和铣削加工

铣削加工包括很多高度灵活的加工操作，使用铣刀和一种在旋转中产生大量切屑的多齿铣刀能够加工各种轮廓外形(见图 7-2)。

(a) 周铣　　　　　(b) 平面铣削　　　　(c) 端铣

图 7-2　铣削加工操作

1．铣削加工

1) 周铣

周铣也称为圆周铣削，在周铣中，刀具的旋转轴线与被加工工件的表面平行(见图 7-2(a))。刀具常用高速钢制造，在圆周方向有一系列的齿，每个齿的工作就如一个单点切削刀具一样，称之为普通切削。

2) 平面铣削

在平面铣削中，刀具安装在主轴上，主轴的旋转轴线与工件表面垂直(见图 7-2(b))。由于切削刀齿和工件之间的相对运动，端铣刀在已加工表面上留下的进给痕迹类似于车削加工留下的痕迹。需要留意的是工件的表面粗糙度取决于刀片的几何角度及每个齿的进给。

3) 端铣

各种类型平面的加工可通过端铣来实现。端铣用的刀具如图 7-2(c)所示，较小或较大尺寸的铣刀带有直的或带锥度的柄部。刀具做旋转运动时，其轴线往往垂直于工件，但它可倾斜来加工锥面。

普通铣削也叫作逆铣，最大切削厚度在刀具的端部(见图 7-3(a))。普通铣削的优点有：①刀齿的啮合并非工件表面特性的功能，②工件表面的杂质和氧化皮不影响刀具寿命。这是比较普通的铣削方式。如果刀具齿形锋利，则加工过程中工件表面是光滑的。然而，刀具有振动的趋势，工件有被向上拉的趋势。因此有必要进行合理的夹紧。

顺铣也叫作同向铣削，切削开始于工件表面，在此屑片是最厚的(见图7-3(b))。优点是切削力向下的部件让工件保持在原位，尤其是对细长的零件。然而，由于当齿轮与工件啮合时导致的高冲击力，此操作必须要有一个刚性的安装支撑，并且必须消除工作台进给机构的后冲。一般来说，在数控机床中，为了延长刀具寿命，推荐采用顺铣。

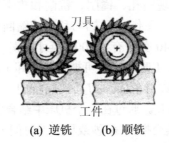

(a) 逆铣   (b) 顺铣

图7-3 逆铣和顺铣的简单示意图

2. 铣床的类型

1) 升降台式铣床

升降台式铣床是最常见的铣床，用于一般的铣削加工。在周铣中，铣刀安装轴是水平安装的，而在平面铣削和端铣、镗削和钻孔加工中铣刀安装轴是垂直安装的。这些铣床的基本部件如下。

工作台，工件在工作台上用T形槽夹紧。工作台相对溜板座纵向移动。

溜板座，它支承工作台并横向移动。

升降台，它支承溜板座并给工作台提供垂直运动，因此切削深度可以调节。

悬臂，在卧式机床中的悬臂可以调节，以适应不同的刀轴长度。

主轴头，它包括主轴和刀具夹持装置。在垂直铣床中，主轴头可固定或垂直方向调节，并且它可在立柱垂直平面旋转加工圆锥面。

2) 卧式铣床

在卧式铣床中，工作台直接安装在床身上，它取代了升降台并只能纵向移动。这类铣床比其他铣床功能少一些，但它们刚性好且用于大批量加工。主轴是水平的或垂直的，并带有两个或三个主轴，用于同时加工两个或三个工件表面。

3) 其他类型的铣床

龙门式铣床，类似于卧式铣床，带有几个主轴头和刀具，可加工多种平面。它们用于加工重型工件，且用于相同任务时在执行刨床更高效。回转工作台铣床类似于立式铣床，且带有一个或多个主轴头，用于平面铣削加工。

通过数控机床，各种铣床部件可快速替换。这些机床功能多样，可进行铣削、钻孔、镗削和攻螺纹，并可保持重复精度。

7.3 加工中心

加工中心是从单个机床发展而来的，单个机床可在人工帮助下完成单个操作，加工中心可完成多个操作。

1968 年，自动换刀的数控机床面世，因此许多不同的操作可在一台机床上完成。这样一台机床被称为"加工中心"——在程序控制下，它能完成许多加工并自动换刀。

加工中心的研究源于数控的历史。数控可以自动编程，机床的某些功能由代码指令控制。

计算机和数控广泛应用于许多机床，从主单轴的钻床(它只能实现两轴控制)，到带有四轴控制的加工中心(它可以实现钻孔、镗削、铣削和攻螺纹等)。一个加工中心可自动选择和交换多达 32 把预设的刀具。工作台可左/右移动或缩回/伸出，且主轴可上/下移动或缩回/伸出，保证定位精度达到每 40 英寸有 0.0003 英寸的误差范围内。机床可自动换刀及自动传送工件。因此，当机床在加工时，工件可被装夹或卸下。

自动换刀的理念扩展到了数控车床。刀具被旋转的刀库夹紧，且龙门式刀库用于换刀。每个刀库夹紧一种典型的刀具。通过在一个机床中结合旋转加工和旋转刀具加工——车削和铣削来实现多功能性。刀具交换在 6 秒或更少的时间内完成。拥有两个或多个工作台是常见的，允许工件被装夹，在机床上完成加工，工作台可自动交换。因此，这些机床的生产效率很高，加工时间常常达到整个时间的 50%。

加工中心有两个新的发展趋势。一个是致力于更小更紧凑的加工中心，另一个是致力于变速或甚至实现无人化操作。在许多公司大量采用现代加工中心来提高生产效率。它们消除了工件从一台机床搬到另一台机床上的无效时间，并消除了工件在单个加工操作中的装卸时间。此外，它们也减少了换刀、执行检测操作及工件在机床上的定位时间。

Technical Reading

Safety Notes for CNC Machine Operations

Safety is always a major concern in a metal-cutting operation. CNC equipment is automated and very fast, and consequently it is a source of hazards. The hazards have to be located and the personnel must be aware of them in order to prevent injuries and damage to the equipment. Main potential hazards includes: rotating parts, such as the spindle, the tool in the spindle, chuck, the part in the chuck, and the turret with the tools and rotating clamping devices; movable parts, such as the machining center table, lathe slides, tailstock center, and tool carousel; errors in the program such as improper use of the G00 code in conjunction with the wrong coordinate value, which can generate an unexpected rapid motion; an error in setting or changing the offset value, which can result in a collision of the tool with the part or the machine; and a hazardous action of the machine caused by unqualified changes in a proven program. To minimize or avoid hazards, try the following preventive actions:

(1) Keep all of the original covers on the machine as supplied by the machine tool builder.

(2) Wear safety glasses, gloves, and proper clothing and shoes.

(3) Do not attempt to run the machine before you are familiar with its control.

(4) Before running the program, make sure that the part is clamped properly.

(5) When proving a program, follow these safety procedures:

- Run the program using the machine LOCK function to check the program for errors in syntax and geometry.
- Slow down rapid motions using the RAPID OVERRIDE switch or dry run the program.
- Use a single-block execution to confirm each line in the program before executing it.
- When the tool is cutting, slow down the feed rate using FEED OVERRIDE switch to prevent excessive cutting conditions.

(6) Do not handle chips by hand and don't use chip hooks to break long curled chips. Program different cutting conditions for better chip control. Stop the machine if you need to properly clean the chips.

(7) If there is any doubt that the insert will break under the programmed cutting conditions, choose a thicker insert or reduce feed or depth of cut.

(8) Keep tool overhang as short as possible, since it can be a source of vibration that can break the insert.

(9) When supporting a large part by the center, make sure that the hole-center is large enough to adequately support and hold the part.

(10) Stop the machine when changing the tools, indexing inserts, or removing chips.

(11) Replace dull or broken tools or inserts.

(12) Write a list of offsets for active tools and clear(set to zero)the offsets for tools removed from the machine.

(13) Do not make changes in the program if your supervisor has prohibited you doing so.

(14) If you have any safety-related concerns, notify your instructor or supervisor immediately.

Unit 8   Computer Aided Design

Computer aided design involves the use of computers to create design drawings and product models. Computer aided design is usually associated with interactive computer graphics, known as a CAD system. This unit mainly introduces CAD system's work, exchange specifications and elements of CAD system.

8.1   CAD System's Work

CAD systems are powerful tools and are used in the design and geometric modeling of components and products.

Drawings are generated at workstations, and the design is displayed continuously on the monitor in different colors for its various components. Designers can easily conceptualize the part designed on the graphics screen and can consider alternative designs or modify a particular design to meet specific design requirements. Using powerful software such as CATIA (computer-aided three-dimensional interactive applications), the design can be subjected to engineering analysis and can identify potential problems, such as excessive load, deflection, or interference at mating surfaces during assembly. Information (such as a list of materials, specifications, and manufacturing instructions) is also stored in the CAD database. Using this information, designer can analyze the manufacturing economics of alternatives.

8.2   Exchange Specifications

Because of the availability of a variety of CAD systems with different characteristics supplied by different vendors, effective communication and exchange of data between these systems are essential. Drawing exchange format (DEX) was developed for use with Autodesk and basically has become a standard because of the long-term success of this software package. DEX is limited to transfer geometry information only. Similarly, stereolithography (STL) formats are used to export three-dimensional geometries, initially only to rapid prototyping system, but recently, it has become a format for data exchange between different CAD systems.

The necessity for a single, neutral format for better compatibility and for the transfer of more information than geometry alone is currently filled mainly by initial graphics exchange specification (IGES). This is used for translation in two directions (in and out of a system) and is also widely used for translation of three-dimensional line and surface data. Because IGES is evolving, there are many variations of IGES.

Another useful format is a solid-model-based standard called the Product Data Exchange Specification (PDES), which is based on the Standard for the Exchange of Product Model Data

(STEP) developed by the International Standard Organization. PDES allows information on shape, design, manufacturing, quality assurance, testing, maintenance, etc., to be transferred between CAD systems.

8.3 Elements of CAD System

The design process in a CAD system consists of the four stages described in this section.

1. Geometric Modeling

In geometric modeling, a physical object or any of its parts is described mathematically or analytically. Designers first construct a geometric model by giving commands that create or modify lines, surfaces, solids, dimensions, and texts. Together, these propose an accurate and complete two or three dimensional representation of the object. The results of these commands are displayed and can be moved around on the screen, and any section desired can be magnified to view details. These data are stored in the database contained in computer memory.

The octree representation of a solid object is shown in Fig. 8-1. It is a three-dimensional analog to pixels on a television screen. Just as any area can be broken down into quadrants, any volume can be broken down into octants, which are then identified as solid, void, or partially filled. Partially filled voxels (from volume pixels) are broken into smaller octants and are reclassified. With increasing resolution, exceptional part detail is achieved. This process may appear to be some what cumbersome, but it allows for accurate description of complex surfaces. It is used particularly in biomedical applications, such as for modeling bone geometries.

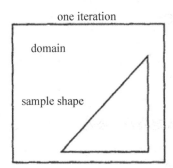
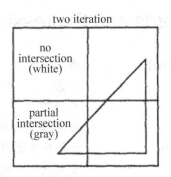
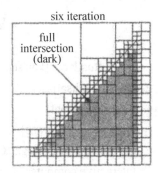

Fig. 8-1 The octree representation of a solid object

The octree representation of a solid object. Any volume can be broken down into octants, which are then identified as solid, void or partially filled. Shown is a two-dimensional version (or quadtree) for the representation of shapes in a plane.

2. Design Analysis and Optimization

After the geometric features of a particular design have been determined, the design is subjected to an engineering analysis. This phase may consist of analyzing (for example) stresses, strains, deflections, vibrations, heat transfer, temperature distribution, or dimensional tolerances. Various sophisticated software packages are available, each having the capabilities to compute these quantities accurately and rapidly.

Because of the relative ease with which such analysis can now be done, designers are increasingly willing to analyze a design more thoroughly before it moves onto production. Experiments and measurements in the field nonetheless maybe necessary to determine the actual effects of loads, temperature, and other variables on the designed components.

3. Design Review and Evaluation

An important design stage is design review and evaluation used to check for any interference between various components. This is done in order to avoid difficulties during assembly or in use of the part and to determine whether moving members (such as linkages) are going to operate as intended. Software is available with animation capabilities to identify potential problems with moving members and other dynamic situations. During the design review and evaluation stage, the part is dimensioned and toleranced precisely to the full degree required for manufacturing it.

4. Documentation and Drafting

After the preceding stages have been completed, the design is reproduced by automated drafting machines for documentation and reference. At this stage, detailed and working drawing are also developed and printed. The CAD system is also capable of developing and drafting sectional views of the part, scaling the drawings, and performing transformations in order to present various views of the part.

Words and Expressions

conceptualize	[kən'septjuəlaiz]	概念化
pixel	['piksəl]	像素
octant	['ɔktənt]	八分圆
tolerance	['tɔlərəns]	给(机器部件等)规定公差，公差
computer-aided design (CAD)		计算机辅助设计
interactive computer graphics		交互式计算机绘图
octree representation		八叉树表示方法
drawing exchange format		图形交换格式
Autodesk 美国电脑软件公司，生产计算机辅助设计软件，如 AutoCAD、3D Studio 等		
stereolithography		光固化快速成型
geometric modeling		几何建模
quadtree		四叉树
initial graphics exchange specification		初始图形交换标准

Notes

(1) Designers can easily conceptualize the part designed on the graphics screen and can consider alternative designs or modify a particular design to meet specific design requirements.

designed on the graphics screen 在此作为 part 的后置定语。

本句可以翻译为：设计人员可以不费力气地在图形屏幕上获得想要设计的零件概念，并能考虑几种可能的设计方案，或者修正某种设计来满足具体的设计要求。

(2) Just as any area can be broken down into quadrants, any volume can be broken down into octants, which are then identified as solid, void, or partially filled.

Just as …在此含义为"正如……"。

句中，由 which 引导的非限定从句修饰前面的内容。

本句可以翻译为：正如任何面积可以分解为四等份一样，任何体积也可以分解为八等份，然后作为实体、空穴或部分填充进行识别。

(3) During the design review and evaluation stage, the part is dimensioned and toleranced precisely to the full degree required for manufacturing it.

dimension 与 tolerance 在本句中作动词，分别解释为"标注所需尺寸"和"规定公差"。

本句可以翻译为：在设计评审与评估阶段，零件被最大程度地标注准确尺寸并规定公差，以满足制造要求。

(4) The CAD system is also capable of developing and drafting sectional views of the part, scaling the drawings, and performing transformations in order to present various views of the part.

be capable of …在此含义为"能够……"。

本句可以翻译为：CAD 系统也能够生成剖面图并进行绘制、缩放，同时也可以进行转换以呈现零件的各种剖面。

Exercises

1. After reading the text above, summarize the main ideas in oral.

2. Fill in the blanks with proper words or phrases according to the text (note the proper tense).

(1) Computer-aided design is usually a_____ interactive computer graphics, known as a CAD system.

(2) The CAD system is also c_____ developing and drafting sectional views of the part, s_____ drawings, and p_____ transformations in order to present various views of the part.

(3) During the design review and evaluation stage, the part is d_____ precisely to the full degree required for manufacturing it.

(4) After the geometric features of a particular design h_____, the design is subjected

to an engineering analysis.

(5) Just as any area can be b_____ quadrants, any volume can be broken down into octants, which are then identified as solid, void, or partially filled.

(6) Designers can easily c_____ the part designed on the graphics screen and can consider a_____ designs or modify a particular design to meet specific design requirements.

3. Translate the following phrases into Chinese according to the text.

(1) CAD
(2) DEX
(3) IGES
(4) ISO
(5) be capable of
(6) be broken down into
(7) be based on
(8) be associated with
(9) consist of
(10) allow for

4．Translate the following phrases into English according to the text.

(1) 几何建模
(2) 几何特征
(3) 软件包
(4) 设计评审
(5) 设计优化
(6) 八叉树表示方法

5. Write a 100-word summary according to the text.

课文参考译文

第8单元 计算机辅助设计

计算机辅助设计包括使用计算机来生成设计图纸和产品模型。计算机辅助设计往往与交互式计算机绘图有关，被称为CAD系统。本单元主要介绍了CAD系统的工作、交换标准以及CAD系统的组成。

8.1 CAD系统的工作

CAD系统是强大的工具，它用于零件和产品的设计与几何建模。图纸在工作站生成，设计的不同零件以不同颜色在显示器上连续显示。设计人员可以不费力气地在图形屏幕上获得想要设计的零件概念，并能考虑几种可能的设计方案，或者修正某种设计来满足具体的设计要求。使用像CATIA(计算机辅助三维交互式应用)这样强大的软件，设计能用来进行工程分析和发现潜在的问题，例如过载、偏斜或装配中配合面的过盈。信息(例如材料清单、标准或加工说明书)也存储在 CAD 数据库中。使用这些信息，设计师可以分析几种可能加工的经济性。

8.2 交换标准

由于不同经销商提供了各种不同特性的 CAD 系统，这些系统间的有效通信和数据交换是十分必要的。由于软件包的长期成功应用，图形交换格式(DEX)被发展用于 Autodesk 且成为一个标准。DEX 仅仅局限于几何信息的传递。类似地，光固化快速成型(STL)形式被用于三维几何信息输出，最初仅用于快速成型系统，但是最近，它变成一种在不同 CAD 系统中交换数据的格式。

为了实现更好的兼容性及不仅仅传递几何信息，单一的中立的格式的必要性目前主要通过初始图形交换标准(IGES)已被满足。这用于两个方向的转换(系统的输入和输出)，并且也广泛应用于三维直线和表面数据的转换。由于 IGES 不断变化发展，因此 IGES 有很多版本。

另一种有用的格式是基于实体模型的标准，称为产品数据交换标准(PDES)，它是基于国际标准组织开发的产品模型数据交换标准(STEP)。PDES 允许形状、设计、制造、质量保证、检测和维护等信息在 CAD 系统中传递。

8.3 CAD 系统的组成

CAD 系统中的设计过程包含本节描述的四个阶段。

1. 几何建模

在几何建模中，一个实际物体或它的任意零件从数学角度或分析角度进行描述。首先，设计师通过创建或修改直线、表面、实体、尺寸和文件等给定命令来创建一个几何模型。结合这些，就提出了物体的准确完整的二维或三维描述。这些命令的结果被显示且能在屏幕上移动，且任何需要的部分可被放大以查看细节。这些数据保存在计算机存储器的数据库中。

实体的八叉树表示方法如图 8-1 所示。它是三维的类似电视屏幕上的像素。"正如任何面积可以分解为四等份一样，任何体积也可以分解为八等份，然后作为实体、空穴或部分填充进行识别。"部分填充体素(voxel，该词源于 volume pixel)被划分成小的八分圆且重新分类。随着不断地改革，可获得特殊部件的细节。这个过程比较烦琐，但它可以精确描述复杂表面。它特别适用于生物医学，如骨骼的几何建模。

2. 设计分析和优化

特定设计的几何特征被确定后，该设计可进行工程分析。这个阶段包括分析(例如)压力、应力、偏斜、振动，热传递、温度分布或尺寸公差。各种复杂的软件包都可被获取，每个软件包都具有准确快速计算上述这些物理量的能力。

由于完成分析相对容易，设计师越来越喜欢在实际生产前更全面地分析设计。但是在该领域实验和检测是必要的，它们用来确定设计零件的负载、温度和其他变量的实际影响。

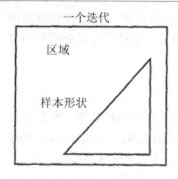 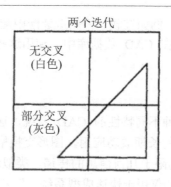 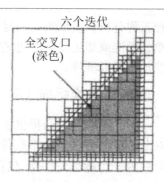

图 8-1 实体的八叉树表示法

3. 设计评审与评估

设计评审是一个重要的设计阶段，用来检查各种零件间有无干涉。做设计评审是为了避免零件装配困难或使用困难，以及确定移动部件(如连杆)是否按预期做运动。软件具有动画地发现在运动部件和其他动态环境下的潜在问题的能力，在设计评审阶段中，零件被最大限度地标注准确尺寸并规定公差，以满足制造要求。

4. 文件存档与绘图

在完成上述阶段后，通过自动绘图仪来重新生成设计，以便于存档和参考。在这一阶段中，局部放大图和工作图也被生成并打印。CAD 系统也能够生成剖面图并进行绘制、缩放，同时也可以进行转换以呈现零件的各种剖面。

Technical Reading

CAD Model Development for Automotive Components

CAD models are used extensively for a great variety of tasks. In the automotive industry, for example, it is especially important to have a detailed CAD model of a particular component in the product database in order to ensure that all of those who will be working on it have all of the data they need to perform their tasks. Special care is taken to build very precise CAD models of the automobile components that passengers will see and interact with on a regular basis. Examples of such components are outer-body panels, handles, seats, and the instrument panel. The quality of the visible (class I) surfaces has a major impact on overall vehicle quality and customer perception of the look and feel of the automobile.

1) Two-dimensional concepts ketches

Stylists with a background and experience in industrial design and/or art first develop two-dimensional concepts through a series of sketches. These sketches are most frequently drawn by hand, although software maybe used instead, especially if the stylist starts with a photograph or a scanned drawing that needs to be modified. Concepts ketches provide an overall feel for the aesthetics of the object and frequently are very detailed and show texture, color, and where individual surfaces on a vehicle should meet. Most often, stylists are given a set of packaging constraints, such as (a) how the component should be assembled with other components, (b) what the size of the component should be, and (c) what the size and shape of any structure lying behind the visible surfaces should be. The time involved in producing a series of such concepts ketches for an individual component or a set of components typically ranges from a few days to several weeks.

2) Three-dimensional surface models

As a concept is being reviewed and refined, several very accurate surface models of the component are constructed. To start the surface model, a computer-controlled optical scanner scans a conceptualized clay model, producing a cloud-of-points organized along the scan lines. Depending on the size of the component, a point cloud may consist of hundreds of thousands to millions of points. The point cloud is read into point-processing software (such as Paraform or ICEM surf) to further organize the points and filter out noise. Scanning can take anywhere from several hours to a day to be completed. If, however, a digital three-dimensional clay model of the component is already available, it is converted into a point cloud organized into scan lines without the need for physical scanning and point-cloud post-processing.

Next, the scan lines from the point cloud are used to construct mathematical surfaces using software, such as ICEM Surf and Alias/Wavefront Studio Tools. To construct the surfaces, first freeform NURBS curves that interpolate or approximate the scan lines are constructed. A NURBS surface patch then is fit through the curves. An individual surface patch models a small region of a single component's face. Several patches are constructed and jointed smoothly at common edges to form the entire face.

Faces join each other at common edges to model an entire component. A great deal of experience is required to determine how to divide a face into a collection of patches that can be fit with the simplest low-order surfaces possible and still meet smoothly at common boundaries. A surfacing specialist performs this task in conjunction with the stylist to ensure that the surfaces are of high quality and that they capture the stylist's intent. A single component may take as long as a week to model.

Surface models are passed along to the various downstream departments to be used for tooling design, feasibility checks, analysis, and for the design of non-visible (class II)surfaces. As the design evolves, the dimensional tolerances on the surfaces are tightened gradually.

When designing outer-body panels, a major milestone is finalizing what is called first flange and fillet, in which the edges of the body panels are turned under or hemmed to provide a flange to connect to the inner panel. The shape of the flange and fillet affects the overall aesthetics and shape of the body panel; hence, their careful design is important. After the shape of the fillet and flange had been decided, the inner-panel designs can be completed.

3) Surface verification

Once the final surface model, which must be verified and evaluated for surface quality and aesthetics, is completed NC tool paths are generated automatically from the surfaces, either from within the surfacing software or through specialized machining software. The tool paths then are used to CNC machine surfaces in clay. If the component is small, instead of machining a clay model, an STL file can be generated and the mock-up can be built on a rapid prototyping machine. It takes anywhere from several hours to several days to machine a component and perform any hand finishing that may be required.

Clay models can be coated with a thin layer of latex material and painted to make them look more realistic and to help evaluate surface quality. The coating may be modified to improve surface smoothness between patches or to change the way light reflects off the surface of the model. All changes made to the clay must be translated back to the digital surface model, either through rescanning and refitting the surface patches or by tweaking the shape of the existing patches.

4) Solid-model construction

After the surface model is finalized, it is used to develop a solid model. For sheet-metal components (such as body panels), body specialists offset the surfaces to form a solid. For other components (such as instrument panels, door handles, or wheels), they add manufacturing features to the surface models (such as flanges, bosses, and ribs). They collaborate with the manufacturers to determine what features must be added and where they should be placed to ensure that the component can be fabricated from the desired material at the target cost.

In the process of making a solid model, it may be discovered that the surface model must be modified because of (a) changes in packaging constraints, (b) the component failing to meet minimal manufacturing requirements, or (c) surfaces not matching up properly at common edges with the appropriate smoothness. These changes are communicated back to the surface modeler and the stylist so that the surfaces can be modified and reverified. Finally, the solid model is entered into a product database where it is then available to suppliers and engineers for further analysis and manufacturing.

Unit 9 Computer Aided Manufacturing and Flexible Manufacturing System

With the advent of computer aided manufacturing (CAM) and flexible manufacturing system (FMS) in manufacturing industry, they obviously increase the productivity. In this unit, it mainly introduces the knowledge of CAM and FMS.

9.1 Computer Aided Manufacturing

Computer aided manufacturing (CAM) started with NC in 1949 at MIT. This project, sponsored by the U.S. Air Force, was the first application of computer technology to control the operation of a milling machine.

Standard NC machines greatly reduced the machining time required to produce a part or complete a production run of parts, but the overall operation was still time-consuming. Tapes had to be prepared for the part, editing the program would result in making a new tape, and tapes had to be rewound each time a part was completed. With this in mind, the machine manufacturers added a computer to the existing NC machine, introducing the beginning of CNC.

The addition of the computer greatly increased the flexibility of the machine tool. The parts' program was now run from the computer's memory instead of from a tape that had to be rewound. Any revisions or editing of the program could be done at the machine, and changes could be stored.

As the machine tool manufacturers continued to improve the efficiency of their machines, the computer capabilities were greatly increased to programmable microprocessors, and many time-saving devices were introduced to increase the machine's cutting time and reduce downtime. Some of these machine options are automatic tool changers, parts' loaders and unloaders, chip conveyors, tool wear monitor, in-process gauging and robots—which brings us to today's machining centers.

CAM uses all the advanced technologies to automate the operations in manufacturing and handle the data that drives the process. The tools of CAM include computer technologies, computer aided engineering (CAE), and robotics. CAM uses all these technologies to join the process of design with automated production machine tools, material handling equipment, and control systems. Without computers, the most important tool in industry, the productivity of the United States would be in serious trouble. Computers help people to become more productive and to do things that would almost be impossible without them.

CAM ties together all the major functions of a factory. The manufacturing or production operations are joined together with the process planning, production scheduling, material handling, inventory control, product inspection, machinery control, and maintenance to form a total manufacturing system.

A CAM system generally contains three major divisions.

Manufacturing: The physical operation of controlling the machine tools, material handling equipment, inspection operations, etc., in order to produce the parts required.

Engineering: The process which involves design and engineering activities to ensure that the parts are designed properly in order to function as required.

Management: The information such as scheduling, inventory control, labor, and manufacturing costs, and all the data required to control the entire plant.

CAM increases the productivity and versatility of machine tools. Before the introduction of NC and CAM, most machine tools were cutting metal only about 5 percent of the time. The automated systems available now cut metal about 70 percent of the time, and the goal is to come as close as possible to having them remove metal 100 percent of the available time.

9.2 Flexible Manufacturing System

The evolution of manufacturing can be represented graphically as a continuum as shown in Fig. 9-1. As this figure shows, manufacturing processes and systems are in a state of transition from manual operation to the eventual realization of fully integrated manufacturing. The step preceding computer-integrated manufacturing is called flexible manufacturing.

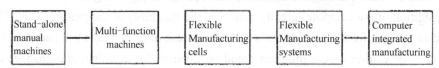

Fig. 9-1 Manufacturing continuum

Flexibility is an important characteristic in modern manufacturing setting. It means that a manufacturing system is versatile and adaptable, while capable of handling relatively high production runs.

A flexible manufacturing system (FMS) is a highly automated GT machine cell, consisting of a group of processing workstations (usually CNC machine tools), interconnected by an automated material handling and storage system. The reason the FMS is called flexible is that it is capable of processing a variety of different part styles simultaneously at the various workstations, and the mix of part styles and quantities of production can be adjusted in response to changing patterns demanded. The FMS is most suited for the mid-variety, mid-volume production range.

These technologies include automated materials handling, group technology, and computer and distributed numerical control. The key elements necessary for a manufacturing system to qualify as an FMS are as follows:

(1) Computer control.

(2) Automated materials handling capability.

(3) Tool handling capability.

Unit 9 Computer Aided Manufacturing and Flexible Manufacturing System

Flexible manufacturing was born in the mid-1960s when the British firm Molins, Ltd. developed its System 24. System 24 is a real FMS. However, it was doomed from the outset because automation, integration, and computer control technology had not yet been developed to the point where they could properly support the system. With the emergency of sophisticated computer control technology in the late 1970s and early 1980s flexible manufacturing became a viable concept. The first major users of flexible manufacturing in the United States were manufacturers of automobiles, trucks, and tractors.

One of the major trends accompanying this shift is the move from design and construction of essentially monolithic systems to modular systems/modular with respect to both hardware and software. Another major worldwide trend is the aim of making an FMS more intelligent. At this stage most of this effort is centered around making the workstations more intelligent. This includes development and application of such features as on-line diagnostics combined with feedback to accomplish self-correction of actual or incipient failures, in-process sensing and feedback control of machining and cutting tool conditions and of the location of workpiece surfaces, and in-process sensing and control of workplace accuracy, surface quality, etc.

Flexible manufacturing takes a major step toward the goal of fully integrated manufacturing by integrating several automated manufacturing concepts:

(1) Computer numerical control (CNC) of individual machine tools.

(2) Distributed numerical control (DNC) of manufacturing systems.

(3) Automated materials handling systems.

(4) Group technology (families of parts).

When these automated processes, machines, and concepts are brought together in one integrated system, an FMS is the result. Humans and computers play major roles in an FMS. The amount of human labor is much less than with a manually operated manufacturing system, of course. However, humans still play a vital role in the operation of an FMS. Human tasks include the following:

(1) Equipment troubleshooting, maintenance and repair.

(2) Tool changing and setup.

(3) Loading and unloading the system.

(4) Data input.

(5) Changing of parts programs.

(6) Development of programs.

An FMS can handle higher volumes and production rates than independent CNC machines. They cannot quite match such machines for flexibility, but they come close. What is particularly significant about the middle ground capabilities of flexible manufacturing is that most manufacturing situations require medium production rates to produce medium volumes with enough flexibility to quickly reconfigure to produce another part or product. Flexible manufacturing fills this long-standing void in manufacturing.

Flexible manufacturing, with its ground capabilities, offers a number of advantages for

机电与数控专业英语

manufacturers:

(1) Flexibility within a family of parts.
(2) Random feeding of parts.
(3) Simultaneous production of different parts.
(4) Decreased setup time and lead time.
(5) More efficient machine usage.
(6) Decreased direct and indirect labor costs.
(7) Ability to handle different materials.
(8) Ability to continue some production if one machine breaks down.

Words and Expressions

flexibility [ˌfleksə'biliti]	灵活性，柔性
revision [ri'viʒin]	修正，修订
microprocessor [ˌmaikrəu'prəusesə]	微处理器
automate ['ɔ:təmeit]	使自动化
versatility [ˌvə:sə'tiliti]	多功能性
CAM (Computer Aided Manufacturing)	计算机辅助制造
CNC (Computer Numerical Control)	计算机数字控制
time-saving	省时的
automatic tool changer	自动换刀架
in-process gauging	在线检测
machine center	加工中心
flexible manufacturing	柔性制造
manufacturing process	加工工艺
mid-variety	中等种类
automated manufacturing system	自动制造系统
mid-volume	中等批量
family of parts	零件族
distributed numerical control	分布式数控
group technology (GT)	成组技术
automated materials handling system	自动化的材料处理系统

Notes

(1) Standard NC machines greatly reduced the machining time required to produce a part or complete a production run of parts, but the overall operation was still time-consuming.

time-consuming 在此翻译为"耗费时间的，费时的"。

本句可以翻译为：标准的数控机床极大地减少了加工单一零件或完成零件整个生产过

Unit 9 Computer Aided Manufacturing and Flexible Manufacturing System

程所需要的加工时间，但整体的操作仍然费时。

(2) As the machine tool manufacturers continued to improve the efficiency of their machines, the computer capabilities were greatly increased to programmable microprocessors, and many time-saving devices were introduced to increase the machine's cutting time and reduce downtime.

as 在此意思为"随着"，time-saving 在此意思是"节省时间的"，与 time-consuming 意思恰好相反。

本句可以翻译为：随着机床生产厂家不断地提高他们的机床效率，计算机上编程微处理器的能力也极大地增强了，引入了很多节省时间的装置，机床的加工时间增加了，停机时间减少了。

(3) It means that a manufacturing system is versatile and adaptable, while also capable of handling relatively high production runs.

It means that …是一个句型，翻译为"它意味着……"

capable of 的意思是"能够……"。

本句可以翻译为：它意味着制造系统用途多且适应性强，同时又能进行较大产量的制造。

(4) A flexible manufacturing system (FMS) is a highly automated GT machine cell, consisting of a group of processing workstations (usually CNC machine tools), interconnected by an automated material handling and storage system.

GT 在此是 group technology，含义是"成组技术，成组工艺"。

本句可以翻译为：柔性制造系统(FMS)是高度自动化的成组工艺加工单元，由一组通过自动化的材料处理和存储系统相连的加工工作站(通常是 CNC 机床)组成。

(5) What is particularly significant about the middle ground capabilities of flexible manufacturing is that most manufacturing situations require medium production rates to produce medium volumes with enough flexibility to quickly reconfigure to produce another part or product.

particularly 在这里是副词，意思是"尤其，特别"。

reconfigure 是在单词"configure"前面加了"re"组成了一个新单词。"re-"表示"再次"，如

  place 放置——replace 替换

  view 观察，观看——review 回顾，复习

  form 形成——reform 改造

本句可以翻译为：柔性制造的中等基本能力的特别优势在于大多数制造要求用中等的生产率来制造中等量的产品，同时用足够的柔性快速重组配置来制造另一个零件或产品。

Exercises

1. Answer the following questions according to the text above.

(1) What is the CAM?

(2) How many tools are there composed of the CAM? What are they?

(3) What is the FMS?

(4) What are the key elements for the FMS?

(5) What is the FMS composed of?

(6) What makes the FMS flexible?

(7) What roles do humans and computers play in the FMS?

2. Translate the following expressions into Chinese.

(1) overall operation

(2) making a new tape

(3) each time a part was completed

(4) the flexibility of the machine tool

(5) improve the efficiency

(6) automatic tool changer

(7) tool wear monitor

(8) computer aided engineering

(9) flexible manufacturing

(10) manufacturing process

(11) automated manufacturing system

(12) group technology

3. Fill in the blanks with the information given in the text.

(1) A CAM system generally contains three major divisions:
_____
_____

(2) A flexible manufacturing system (FMS) is a highly automated GT machine cell consisting of_____.

(3) The key elements necessary for a manufacturing system to qualify as an FMS are as follows:
_____
_____

(4) Flexible manufacturing takes a major step toward the goal of fully integrated manufacturing by integrating several automated manufacturing concepts:
_____
_____

4. Decide whether the following statements are True (√) or False (×) according to the information of the text.

(1) The CAM started with the emerge of the NC.　　　　　　　　　　　(   )

Unit 9 Computer Aided Manufacturing and Flexible Manufacturing System

(2) FMS is the eventual realization of full integrated manufacturing.　　　　　(　　)

(3) A flexible manufacturing is versatile because it can produce different kinds of parts. (　　)

(4) Human tasks in an FMS are confined to the machine maintenance, trouble shooting and monitoring so FMS liberate humans from labor.　　　　　　　　　　　(　　)

(5) FMS is mainly used in the manufacture of autos, trucks and tractors.　　(　　)

(6) It is only with the emergency of sophisticated computer control technology that an FMS is possible.　　　　　　　　　　　　　　　　　　　　　　　　　　　(　　)

5. Write a 100-word summary according to the text.

课文参考译文

第9单元　计算机辅助制造与柔性制造系统

随着计算机辅助制造(CAM)及柔性制造系统(FMS)在加工制造工业的出现，它们明显提高了生产效率。本单元介绍了计算机辅助制造及柔性制造系统的一些知识。

9.1　计算机辅助制造

计算机辅助制造(CAM)是1949年在麻省理工学院随着数控的发展而出现的。由美国空军发起的这一项目，是计算机技术控制铣削加工的第一次应用。

标准的数控机床极大地减少了加工单一零件或完成零件整个生产过程所需要的加工时间，但整体的操作仍然费时。必须为零件准备纸带，编辑程序将导致产生一个新纸带，且每次加工完零件后，纸带必须倒回。考虑到这些，机床生产者把计算机引入现有的数控机床，计算机数控便出现了。

计算机的引入极大地增加了机床的柔性。目前，零件加工程序是由计算机存储器提供，而不是由必须被卷回的纸带提供。在机床上可以完成任何程序的修正和编辑，修改后的程序也能存储。

随着机床生产厂家不断地提高他们的机床效率，计算机上编程微处理器的功能也极大地增强了，引入了很多节省时间的装置，机床的加工时间增加了，停机时间减少了。这些装置包括自动换刀、零件自动装卸、切屑自动传输、自动监控刀具磨损、在线检测和机器人等——这就产生了现在的加工中心。

在自动加工和处理生产中的数据方面，CAM完全采用先进技术。CAM的工具包括计算机技术、计算机辅助工程(CAE)及机器人技术。CAM使用所有的这些技术把设计过程和自动加工机床、材料处理设备及控制系统连接起来。如果没有计算机——这个工业中最重要的工具，美国的生产力将陷入严重的困境。计算机使人们提高生产效率，帮助人们完成了离开计算机就几乎不能完成的事情。

CAM集中了工厂所有主要的功能。它把制造或生产运营和工艺规划、生产调度、材料处理、报表控制、产品检验、机器控制及维修连在一起，形成一个完整的加工系统。

CAM系统一般包括三个主要的部分。

制造：是对机床控制、材料处理设备、检测运行等的实际操作，目的就是加工所需要的零件。

工程：是涉及设计和工程行为的工艺，目的就是确保零件设计合理，并达到所要求的功能。

管理：是对计划、报表控制、劳力、加工成本等信息以及控制整个工厂需要的所有数据进行管理。

CAM 提高了机床的生产率，增强了机床的功能。在 NC 和 CAM 引入以前，大多数机床的加工时间只占总时间的 5%。现有的自动加工系统加工时间占总时间的 70%。我们的目标是要使他们的切削时间尽可能接近总时间 100%。

9.2 柔性制造系统

制造的发展过程可用图表示为一个连续统一体，如图 9-1 所示。从图上可以看出，制造的过程和系统处在由手工操作到最后实现全面的集成制造的过渡状态。计算机集成制造的前一步叫作柔性制造。

图 9-1 制造的连续统一体

柔性是现代制造环境中一个重要的特征。它意味着制造系统用途多且适应性强，同时又能进行较大产量的制造。

柔性制造系统(FMS)是高度自动化的成组工艺加工单元，由一组通过自动化的材料处理和存储系统相连的加工工作站(通常是 CNC 机床)组成。柔性制造系统之所以称为柔性是因为它能在各工作站同时加工许多不同类型的零件，并且可以根据所需类型的变化来混合零件的种类和调整产品的数量。柔性制造系统最适合于中等种类和中等批量的生产范围。

这些工业技术包括自动化的材料处理、成组技术及计算机和分布式数字控制。一个制造系统要成为柔性制造系统必须具备的要素如下。

(1) 计算机控制。

(2) 自动化材料处理能力。

(3) 刀具处理能力。

柔性制造产生于 20 世纪 60 年代中期，当时英国莫林斯有限公司开发了 24 号系统。24 号系统是一个真正的 FMS。然而，它从一开始就注定是失败的，因为自动化、集成化和计算机控制技术还没有发展到能够恰当地支持这一系统的程度。随着复杂计算机控制技术在 20 世纪 70 年代末和 80 年代初的出现，柔性制造才成为可能。在美国柔性制造系统最初的主要用户是汽车、卡车和拖拉机制造商。

伴随这个转变的主要趋势之一是把基本的单块集成电路的设计和结构转到模块系统——关于硬件和软件的模块。另一个全球化的趋势是使柔性制造系统更智能化。这个阶段主要致力于使工作站更智能化。这包含着诸如对目前或初始故障进行自我修正的与反馈相连的在线诊断特征的开发和应用，机床和刀具条件、工件表面位置的过程传感和反馈控制以及

Unit 9 Computer Aided Manufacturing and Flexible Manufacturing System

车间精度、表面质量等的过程传感和控制。

通过综合几个自动化的制造观念，可以看出，柔性制造系统向全面集成化的制造目标迈出了重要的一步，这些观念如下。

(1) 独立机床的计算机数字控制(CNC)。
(2) 制造系统的分布式数字控制(DNC)。
(3) 自动化的材料处理系统。
(4) 成组技术(零件族)。

当这些自动化工艺、机器和观念合成到一个集成的系统时，就产生柔性制造系统。在柔性制造系统中，人和计算机起了重要作用。当然人的劳动量比手工操作的制造系统要小得多。然而，人仍然在柔性制造系统的操作中起着至关重要的作用。人的任务包括以下几个方面。

(1) 设备故障检测、维护和修理。
(2) 刀具的变换和装配。
(3) 安装和拆卸系统。
(4) 数据输入。
(5) 零件加工程序的变换。
(6) 程序的开发。

柔性制造系统比独立的计算机数控机床具有更大的生产能力和更高的生产率。它们在柔性方面比不上计算机数控机床，但它们相差不多。柔性制造的中等基本能力的特别优势在于大多数制造要求用中等的生产率来制造中等量的产品，同时用足够的柔性快速重组配置来制造另一个零件或产品。柔性制造填补了制造中长期存在的空白。

柔性制造以其基本能力给制造者提供了如下的多个优点。

(1) 在一个零件族内具有柔性。
(2) 随意进给零件。
(3) 同时生产不同的零件。
(4) 准备时间以及从产品设计到投产的时间减少了。
(5) 机床的使用更有效。
(6) 直接和间接的人力成本减少了。
(7) 能加工不同的材料。
(8) 如果有一台机床出故障仍能进行部分生产。

Technical Reading

Flexible Manufacturing System

The most publicized type of modern manufacturing systems is known as the flexible manufacturing system. The development of FMS began in the United States in the 1960s. The idea was to combine the high reliability and productivity of the transfer line with the programmable flexibility of the NC machine in order to be able to produce a variety of parts. In the late 1960s, such a system was installed for machining aircraft speed drive housings that is still in use today. However, very few of these systems were sold until the late 1970s and early 1980s, when a worldwide FMS movement began.

The FMS is fundamentally an automated, conveyorized, computerized job shop. The system is complex to schedule. Because the machining time for different parts varies greatly, the FMS is difficult to link to an integrated system and often remains an island of expensive automation.

Some common features of FMS are pallet changers, underfloor conveyor systems for the collection of chips, and a conveyor system that delivers parts to the machine.

An FMS system can usually monitor piece part counts, tool changes, and machine utilization, with the computer providing supervisory control of the production. The workpieces are launched randomly into the system, which identifies each part in the family and routes it to the proper machines. The systems generally display reduced manufacturing lead time, low in-process inventory, and high machine tool utilization, with reduced direct and indirect labor. The materials handling system must be able to route any part to any machine in any order and provide each machine with a small queue of "banked parts" waiting to be processed so as to maximize machine utilization. Convenient access for loading and unloading parts, compatibility with the control system, and accessibility to the machine tools are other necessary design features for the materials handling system. The computer control for an FMS system has three levels. The master control monitors the entire system for tool failures or machine breakdowns, schedules the work, and routes the parts to the appropriate machine.

An FMS generally needs about three or four workers per shift to load and unload parts, change tools, and perform general maintenance. The workers in the FMS are usually highly skilled and trained in NC and CNC.

Unit 10　Computer-integrated Manufacturing Systems

Computer-integrated manufacturing (CIM) is the term used to describe the modern approach to manufacturing. Although CIM encompasses many of the other advanced manufacturing technologies such as computer numerical control (CNC), computer-aided design/computer-aided manufacturing (CAD/CAM), robotics, and just-in-time delivery (JIT), it is more than a new technology or a new concept. Computer-integrated manufacturing is an entirely new approach to manufacturing.

10.1　Introduction

The various levels of automation in manufacturing operations have been extended further by increasing information processing functions, utilizing an extensive network of interactive computers. The result is computer-integrated manufacturing, which is a broad term describing the computerized integration of all aspects of design, planning, manufacturing, distribution, and management.

CIM is a methodology and a goal, rather than an assemblage of equipment and computers. The effectiveness of CIM critically depends on the use of a large-scale integrated communications system involving computers, machines, and their controls. Because CIM ideally should involve the total operation of a company, it must have an extensive database concerning technical and business aspects of the operation. Consequently, if implemented all at once, CIM can be prohibitively expensive, particularly for small and medium-sized companies.

Implementation of CIM in existing plants may begin with modules in various phases of the total operation. For new manufacturing plants, on the other hand, comprehensive and long-range strategic planning covering all phases of the operation is essential in order to fully benefit from CIM. Such plans must take into account the following considerations:
- Availability of financial, technical, and human resources;
- The mission, goals, and culture of the organization;
- Existing as well as emerging technologies in the areas of the products to be manufactured;
- The level of integration desired.

10.2　Subsystems of CIM

CIM systems consist of subsystems that are integrated into a whole. These subsystems consist of the following (see Fig.10-1):

- Business planning and support;
- Product design;
- Manufacturing process planning;
- Process automation and control;
- Shop floor monitoring systems.

The subsystems are designed, developed, and implemented in such a manner that the output of one subsystem serves as the input of another subsystem. Organizationally, these subsystems usually are divided into two functions.

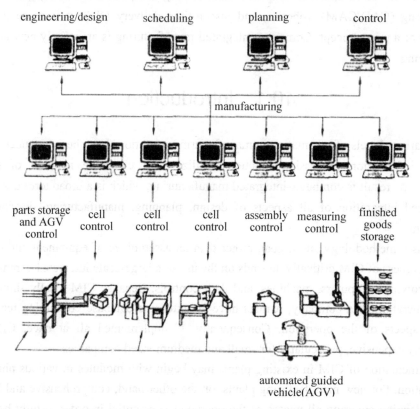

Fig.10-1 A schematic illustration of a computer-integrated manufacturing system

- Business planning functions: These include activities such as forecasting, scheduling, material-requirements planning, invoicing, and accounting.
- Business execution functions: Include production and process control, material handling, testing, and inspection of the system.

The major benefits of CIM are as follows.

- Emphasis on product quality and uniformity, as implemented through better process control.
- Efficient use of materials, machinery, and personnel and major reduction of work-in-progress inventory, all of which improve productivity and lower product cost.

- Total control of the production, schedules, and management of the entire manufacturing operation.
- Responsiveness to shorter product life cycles, changing market demands, and global competition.

10.3　Database

An efficient CIM system requires a single database to be shared by the entire manufacturing organization. A database consists of up-to-date, detailed, and accurate information relating to products, designs, machines, processes, materials, production, finances, purchasing, sales, marketing, and inventory. This vast array of data is stored in computer memory and recalled or modified as necessary either by individuals in the organization or by the CIM system itself, while it is controlling various aspects of design and production. A database generally consists of the following items, some of which are classified as technical and others as nontechnical.

- Product data: part shape, dimensions, and specifications.
- Data management attributes: revision level, and part number.
- Production data: manufacturing processes used.
- Operational data: scheduling, lot sizes, and assembly requirements.
- Resources data: capital, machines, equipment, tooling personnel, and their capabilities.

Databases are built by individuals and by the use of various sensors in the production machinery and equipment. Data are collected automatically by a data-acquisition system (DAS), which can report the number of parts being produced per unit of time, their dimensional accuracy, surface finish, weight, and other characteristics at specified rates of sampling.

The components of DAS include microprocessors, transducers, and analog-to-digital converters (ADCs). Data-acquisition systems are also capable of analyzing the data and transferring them to other computers for purposes such as statistical analysis, data presentation, and the forecasting of product demand. Several factors are important in the use and implementation of databases.

- They should be timely, accurate, easily accessible, easily shared, and user-friendly.
- Because it is used for various purposes and by many people, the database must be flexible and responsive to the needs of different uses.
- CIM systems can be accessed by designers, manufacturing engineers, process planners, financial officers, and the management of the company by using appropriate access codes. Of course, companies must protect data against tampering or unauthorized use.
- If there are problems with data accuracy, the correct data should be recovered and restored.

10.4　The CIM Wheel

The Computer and Automated Systems Association (CASA) of the Society of Manufacturing Engineers(SME) developed the CIM wheel (see Fig. 10-2) as a way to comprehensively but concisely illustrate the concept of CIM. The CASA/SME developed the CIM wheel to include several distinct components:

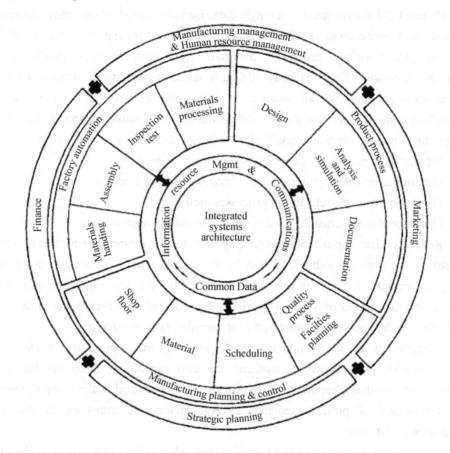

Fig. 10-2　CASA/SME CIM wheel

- Manufacturing management/human resource management;
- Marketing;
- Strategic planning;
- Finance;
- Product/process design and planning;
- Manufacturing planning and control;
- Factory automation.

Unit 10 Computer-integrated Manufacturing System

Words and Expressions

methodology	[ˌmeθə'dɔlədʒi]	操作法，方法学，工艺
specification	[ˌspesifi'keiʃən]	说明书，技术要求
assemblage	[ə'semblidʒ]	(机器的)安装，装配
prohibitively	[prəu'hibitivli]	禁止地，(费用)过高地，过分地
concisely	[kən'saisli]	简明扼要地
comprehensive	[ˌkɔmpri'hensiv]	全面的，广泛的
mission	['miʃən]	宗旨，任务，天职
invoice	['invɔis]	发票，发货单，货物
uniformity	[ˌjuːni'fɔːmiti]	均匀性，均匀度，一致性
inventory	['invəntri]	详细目录，存货
statistical	[stə'tistikəl]	统计的，统计学的
shop floor		生产场所
work-in-progress		在制品
computer-integrated manufacturing		计算机集成制造
data-acquisition system (DAS)		数据采集系统
analog-to-digital converter (ADC)		模拟-数字转换器
CASA (Computer and Automated System Association)		(美)计算机与自动化系统协会
up-to-date		最近的，最新状态的，文件内容更新的
SME (Society of Manufacturing Engineers)		(美)制造工程师学会

Notes

(1) The various levels of automation in manufacturing operations have been extended further by increasing information processing functions, utilizing an extensive network of interactive computers.

automation 为句中主语，have been extended 为谓语部分，由 by 引导的两个并列动名词短语 increasing information processing functions 和 utilizing an extensive network of interactive computers 作状语。

本句可以翻译为：在制造加工操作中，各种自动化水平通过增加信息处理功能，使用交互式计算机的扩展网络功能，已经得到了进一步扩展。

(2) Because CIM ideally should involve the total operation of a company, it must have an extensive database concerning technical and business aspects of the operation.

concerning 在这里是介词，意思是"关于，涉及，就……来说"，concerning the matter 的意思是"关于那件事"。

本句可以翻译为：理想的 CIM 应该包括一个公司所有的运转操作，因此它必须要有涉及操作过程的技术上和经营上的一个非常大的数据库。

(3) For new manufacturing plants, on the other hand, comprehensive and long-range strategic planning covering all phases of the operation is essential in order to fully benefit from CIM.

on the other hand 在此含义为"另一方面"。

in order to 在此含义为"得益于，获益于"。

benefit from 在此含义为"为了"。

本句可以翻译为：另一方面，对于新的制造厂家，为了最大限度地获益于 CIM 技术，涵盖工厂运作的所有方面的广泛的、长期的策略计划是必需的。

(4) The subsystems are designed, developed, and implemented in such a manner that the output of one subsystem serves as the input of another subsystem.

in a manner 是介词短语，在此含义是"以……的方式"。

本句可以翻译为：子系统的设计、开发和实现要按照一个子系统的输出作为另一个子系统的输入这样的模式来进行。

(5) This vast array of data is stored in computer memory and recalled or modified as necessary either by individuals in the organization or by the CIM system itself, while it is controlling various aspects of design and production.

while 引导的从句中的 it 仍指 this vast array of data。

本句可以翻译为：这么多的数据存储在计算机的存储器中，需要时由机构中的个人或 CIM 系统本身重新调用或改动，同时它也控制着设计和生产中的各个方面。

Exercises

1. After reading the text above, summarize the main ideas in oral.

2. Fill in the blanks with proper words or phrases according to the text (note the proper tense).

(1) Computer-integrated manufacturing is abroad term describing the computerized integration of all aspects of d_____, p_____, m_____, d_____, and m_____.

(2) Computer-integrated manufacturing systems consist of subsystems such as: b_____, p_____, m_____, p_____and s_____ .

(3) These subsystems usually are divided into two functions: b_____and b_____.

(4) Databases are built by i_____, and by the use of v_____, in the production machinery and equipment. Data are collected automatically by a d_____.

(5)The components of DAS include m_____, t_____, and a_____.

Unit 10 Computer-integrated Manufacturing System

3. Translate the following phrases into Chinese according to the text.

(1) statistical analysis
(2) access codes
(3) process planning
(4) shop floor
(5) ADC
(6) DAS
(7) dimensional accuracy
(8) rates of sampling in the production
(9) material-requirements planning
(10) extensive network of interactive computers
(11) large-scale integrated communications system

4. Translate the following phrases into English according to the text.

(1) 信息处理功能
(2) 长期的策略计划
(3) 人力资源
(4) 存货清单
(5) 车间监控系统
(6) 单位时间内生产的零件数
(7) 表面光洁度
(8) 统计分析
(9) 产品需求预测

5. Translate the following sentences into Chinese.

(1) The result is computer-integrated manufacturing, which is a broad term describing the computerized integration of all aspects of design, planning, manufacturing, distribution, and management.

(2) The subsystems are designed, developed, and implemented in such a manner that the output of one subsystem serves as the input of another subsystem.

(3) CIM systems can be accessed by designers, manufacturing engineers, process planners, financial officers, and the management of the company by using appropriate access codes.

(4) Databases are built by individuals and by the use of various sensors in the production machinery and equipment.

6. Give short answers according to the text.

(1) What is CIMS?
(2) What are the subsystems of Computer-integrated manufacturing systems constituted by?
(3) How many functions of the subsystems of CIMS are described in the text? What are they?

(4) What are the major benefits of CIM?

7. Write a 100-word summary according to the text.

课文参考译文

第 10 单元　计算机集成制造系统

计算机集成制造(CIM)是用来描述现代加工方式的一种术语。尽管 CIM 包括很多其他先进制造技术，例如计算机数字控制(CNC)、计算机辅助设计/计算机辅助制造(CAD/CAM)、机器人技术和准时交货(JIT)，但它不仅仅是一种新技术或新概念。计算机集成制造是一种全新的生产方式。

10.1　简介

在制造加工操作中，各种自动化水平通过增加信息处理功能，使用交互式计算机的扩展网络功能，已经得到了进一步扩展。结果出现了计算机集成制造这个广泛的术语，它描述了设计、计划、制造、分配和管理的各个方面的计算机集成。

CIM 是一个理念和目标，而不是设备和计算机的集成。CIM 的高效性关键取决于包括计算机、机床和它们控制的大规模集成通信系统的使用。理想的 CIM 应该包括一个公司所有的运转操作，因此它必须要有涉及操作过程的技术上和经营上的一个非常大的数据库。因此，一次实现计算机集成制造会特别昂贵尤其是对于中小型企业。

CIM 在现有工厂的实现可以用整个操作的各个阶段为模块开始。另一方面，对于新的制造厂家，为了最大限度地获益于 CIM 技术，涵盖工厂运作的所有方面的广泛的、长期的策略计划是必需的。这些计划必须考虑以下几点。
- 资金、技术、人力资源的获取；
- 组织的宗旨、目标和文化；
- 产品加工领域现有的及新兴的技术；
- 理想的集成水平。

10.2　CIM 的子系统

CIM 系统包括一些子系统，这些子系统集成成为一个整体。这些子系统(参见图 10-1)包括：
- 经营计划与支持；
- 产品设计；
- 加工工艺计划；
- 工艺自动化及控制；
- 车间监控系统。

子系统的设计、开发和实现要按照一个子系统的输出作为另一个子系统的输入这样的模式来进行。就其组织结构来看，这些子系统通常划分为两大功能。

Unit 10　Computer-integrated Manufacturing System

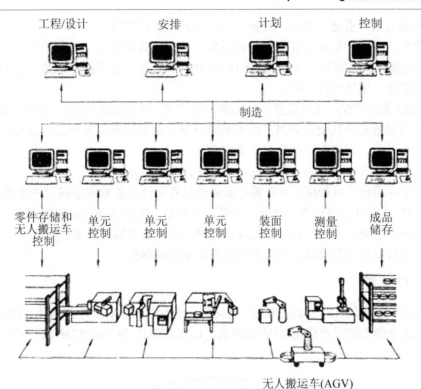

图 10-1　计算机集成制造系统的示意框图

- 经营计划功能：包括预测、调度、物料需求计划、发货和报账等活动。
- 经营执行功能：包括产品和工艺控制、材料处理、检测和系统测试。

计算机集成制造的优点如下。

- 通过实现更好的过程控制，注重产品的质量和一致性。
- 高效地使用材料、设备和人员，以及降低在制品存货量，提高了生产率，降低了产品成本。
- 整个制造操作的生产、调度、管理的整体控制。
- 对更短的产品生命周期、不断变化的市场需求和全球化竞争的响应性。

10.3　数据库

一个高效的 CIM 系统需要一个独立的数据库来给整个制造组织共享。数据库包括有关产品、设计、机床、工艺、材料、生产、资金、采购、销售、市场和存货的最新的、详细而又准确的信息。这么多的数据存储在计算机的存储器中，需要时由机构中的个人或 CIM 系统本身重新调用或改动，同时它也控制着设计和生产中的各个方面。一个数据库主要包括以下技术性的和非技术性的内容。

- 产品数据：零件的形状、尺寸、技术要求。
- 数据管理属性：修改水平和零件编号。
- 生产数据：制造过程中使用。
- 操作数据：调度、批量大小和装配要求。

- 资源数据：资金、机床、设备、刀具人员以及它们的能力。

通过在生产机器和设备上使用各种传感器，数据库就被建立了。数据通过数据采集系统(DAS)来收集，该系统能报告在指定的采样率中单位时间生产的零件数、它们的尺寸精度、表面光洁度、重量和其他特性。

DAS 的组成部件有：微处理器、传感器、模拟-数字转换器(ADC)。数据采集系统也能分析数据并传递数据给其他计算机，用于系统分析、数据显示以及产品需求预测。在数据库的使用和执行中，有几个因素是十分重要的。

- 它们应该及时、准确、易获取、易共享以及用户友好。
- 由于它用途广且使用者多，数据库必须具有柔性且能响应不同用户的需求。
- CIM 系统可由设计者、制造工程师、工艺员、财务人员和公司管理人员使用正确的口令访问。当然，公司必须保护数据，防止数据损坏或未被授权使用数据。
- 如果数据精度有问题，正确的数据应该覆盖并存储。

10.4 CIM 轮

美国制造工程师学会(SME)的计算机与自动化系统协会(CASA)发明了 CIM 轮(见图 10-2)，作为一种方式全面而简明地描述 CIM 的概念，CASA/SME 发明的 CIM 轮包括几个不同组成部分。

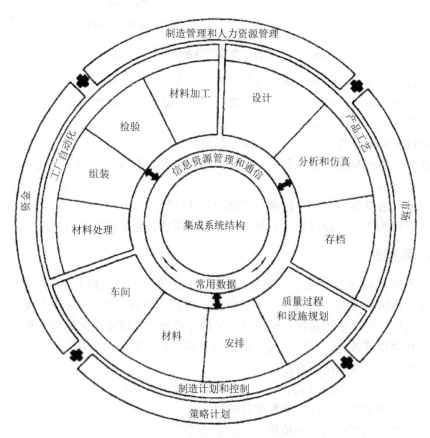

图 10-2　CASA/SME CIM 轮

- 制造管理/人力资源管理；
- 市场；
- 策略计划；
- 资金；
- 产品/工艺设计和计划；
- 制造计划和控制；
- 工厂自动化。

Technical Reading

CIM

1. Introduction

To understand CIM, it is necessary to begin with a comparison of modern and traditional manufacturing. Modern manufacturing encompasses all of the activities and processes necessary to convert raw materials into finished products, deliver them to the market, support them in the market, and support them in the field. These activities include the following:

- Identifying a need for a product;
- Designing a product to meet the needs;
- Obtaining the raw materials needed to produce the product;
- Applying appropriate processes to transform the raw materials into finished products;
- Transporting finished products to the market;
- Maintaining the product to ensure proper performance in the field.

This broad, modern view of manufacturing can be compared with the more limited traditional view that focused almost entirely on the conversion processed. The old approach excluded such critical pre-conversion elements as market analysis research, development, and design as well as after-conversion elements such as product delivery and product maintenance. In other words, in the old approach of manufacturing, only those processes that took place on the shop floor were considered manufacturing. This traditional approach of separating the overall concept into numerous stand-alone specialized elements was not fundamentally changed with the advent of automation.

With CIM, not only are the various elements automated, but the islands of automation are all linked together or integrated. Integration means that a system can provide complete and instantaneous sharing of information. In modern manufacturing, integration is accomplished by computers, CIM, then, is the total integration of all components involved in converting raw materials into finished products and getting the products to the market, as shown in Fig.10-3.

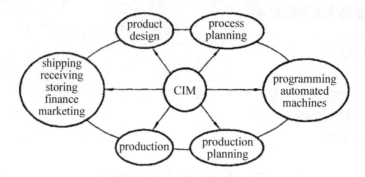

Fig. 10-3 Major components of CIM

2. Historical Development of CIM

The term computer-integrated manufacturing was developed in 1974 by Joseph Harrionton who wrote about tying islands of automation together through the use of computers as the title of a book. It has taken many years for CIM to develop as a concept, but integrated manufacturing is not really new. In fact, integration is where manufacturing actually began. Manufacturing has evolved through four distinct stages.

1) Manual manufacturing

Manual manufacturing using simple hand tools was actually integrated manufacturing. All information needed to design, produce, and deliver a product was readily available because it resided in the mind of the person who performed all of the necessary tasks. The tool of integration in the earliest years of manufacturing was the human mind of the craftsman who designed, produced, and delivered the product. An example of integrated manual manufacturing is the village blacksmith producing a special tool for a local farmer. The blacksmith would have in his mind all of the information needed to design, produce, and deliver the farmer's tools. In this example, all elements of manufacturing are integrated.

2) Mechanization/Specialization

With the advent of the industrial revolution, manufacturing processes became both specialized and mechanized. Instead of one person designing, producing, and delivering a product, workers and/or machines performed specialized tasks within each of these broad areas. Communication among these separate entities was achieved by using drawings, specifications, job orders, process plans, and a variety of other communication aids. To ensure that the finished product could match the planned product, the concept of quality control was introduced.

The advantage of the mechanization/specialization stage was that it permitted mass production interchangeability of parts, different levels of accuracy, and uniformity. The disadvantage is that the lack of integration led to a great deal of waste.

3) Automation

Automation improved the performance and enhanced the capabilities of both people and machines within specialized manufacturing components. For example, CAD enhanced the capability of designers and drafters. CNC enhanced the capabilities of machinists and computer-assisted planners. But the improvements brought on by automation were isolated within individual components or islands. Because of this, automation did not always live up to its potential.

To understand the limitations of automation with regard to overall productivity improvement, consider the following analogy. Suppose that various subsystems of an automobile (i.e., the engine, steering, and brake) were automated to make the driver's job easier. Automatic acceleration, deceleration, steering, and braking would certainly be more efficient than the manual versions. However, consider what would happen if these various automated subsystems were not tied together in a way that allowed them to communicate and share accurate, up-to-date information instantly and continually. One system might attempt to accelerate the automobile while another system was attempting to apply the brakes. The same limitations apply in an automated manufacturing setting. These limitations are what led to the current stage in the development of manufacturing integration.

4) Integration

With the advent of the computer age, manufacturing has developed full circle. It began as a totally integrated concept and, with CIM, has once again become one. However, there are major differences in the manufacturing integration of today and that of the manual era of the past. First, the instrument of integration in the manual era was the human mind. The instrument of integration in modern manufacturing is the computer. Second, processes in the modern manufacturing setting are still specialized and automated.

Another way to view the historical development of CIM is by examining the ways in which some of the individual components of CIM have developed over the years. Such components as designing, planning, and production have evolved both in processes and in the tools and equipment used to accomplish the processes.

Design has evolved from a manual process using tools such as slide rules, triangles, pencils, scales, and erasers into an automated process known as CAD. Process planning has evolved from a manual process using planning tables, diagrams, and charts into an automated process known as CAPP. Production has evolved from a manual process involving manually controlled machines into an automated process known as computer-aided manufacturing (CAM).

These individual components of manufacturing evolved over the years onto separate islands of automation. However, communication among these islands was still handled manually. This limited the level of improvement in productivity that could be accomplished in the overall manufacturing process. When these islands and other automated components of manufacturing are linked together through computer networks, these limitations can be overcome.

Unit 11 Nontraditional Machining Processes

Nontraditional machining process is also called "Special machining process" or "modern machining process", it generally refers to the processing method which uses electric energy, heat energy, light energy, electrochemical energy, chemical energy, sound energy and special mechanical energy and other energy to remove or add materials, thus realizing the materials to be removed, deformation, change in performance or plating, etc. In this unit, it mainly introduces electrical discharge machining (EDM), electrochemical machining (ECM), ultrasonic machining (USM), laser beam machining (LBM), and development trends in the field of machining by cutting and by erosion.

11.1 Electrical Discharge Machining

Electrical discharge machining(EDM) removes metal by controlled electrical arcing (sparking) between the tool and workpiece. The EDM process is valued for its ability to machine complex shapes in metal of any hardness. It is used widely in making injection and compression molds for rubber and plastic molding, molds for die-casting metals, and dies for forging and metal stamping. Because no tool pressures are involved, the process is ideal for machining delicate workpiece.

It is known to every machinist that on standard machine tools electrical energy is converted by an electric motor. Recently, we have discovered that electrical energy can be directly employed in metal removal. The main advantage is that metal of any hardness can be machined by electrical machining processes with good surface finish.

Electrical discharge machining is a form of metal removal in which pulsating direct current is applied to a shaped tool (electrode) and a workpiece, both of which are capable of conducting electricity. The two are held close to each other with a non-conducting fluid serving as an insulator between them. When a voltage high enough to break down the insulator is reached, a spark jumps the gap between the tool and the workpiece. As a result, this spark removes a small portion of material (see Fig. 11-1).

The surface finish of a part produced on an EDM machine depends on the size of the sparks generated between it and the electrode. Fig.11-1 illustrates how big, powerful sparks produce a rough surface and small, less powerful sparks produce a smooth surface. It is reported that metal removal rates and surface finish are controlled by the frequency and intensity of the spark. High frequency, low intensity sparks result in a low metal removal rate and produce a smooth finish. Low frequency, high intensity sparks result in a rapid metal corrosion rate and a coarse finish.

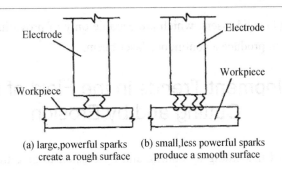

(a) large,powerful sparks create a rough surface

(b) small,less powerful sparks produce a smooth surface

Fig. 11-1 The EDM Process

11.2 Electrochemical Machining

In electrochemical machining(ECM), the tool is the cathode and the workpiece is the anode. A gap of 0.0254 mm to 0.76 mm is maintained between the tool and workpiece. This provides space for the flow of the electrolyte and keeps the electrical circuit from shorting out. A low-voltage, high amperage direct current passes from the workpiece to the tool through electrolyte. This current dissolves metal particles from the workpiece into the electrolyte by electrochemical reaction. The ECM process can be used to machine any metal that conducts electricity, regardless of hardness. The absence of tool pressures on the workpiece makes the process ideal for machining thin metals and fragile workpieces.

11.3 Ultrasonic Machining

In ultrasonic machining (USM), also called impact grinding, fine abrasive particles suspended in a fluid (usually water) are pumped into a gap between the workpiece and the tool. The tool is made to vibrate a few hundredths of a millimeter at ultrasonic frequencies ranging from 19 kHz to 25 kHz. The rapid pumping action of the tool hurls the abrasive particles at the workpiece at high velocity, thus grinding the workpiece to the shape of the tool. A major advantage of USM is that it can machine materials that cannot conduct electricity and which, therefore, cannot be machined by EDM or ECM. However, tool wear is high in USM, due to the abrasive cutting action. One or more roughing tools and a finishing tool are usually required for each job. Tools made of cold-rolled steel or stainless steel provide the best wear ratios.

11.4 Laser Beam Machining

The energy source for laser beam machining(LBM) is a highly concentrated beam of light. When the beam is focused on a small spot, its power density is raised to produce sufficient heat to vaporize any material. However, the rate of metal removal is very small, which limits the use of lasers to hole drilling and cutting operations in relatively thin materials. Two types of lasers are now in common use: (1) solid lasers, which are capable only of providing short bursts of power, and (2) gas lasers, which produce a continuous laser beam.

11.5 Development Trends in the Field of Machining by Cutting and by Erosion

It is the purpose of machining by cutting and by erosion to give the workpiece the desired shape and dimensions of necessary accuracy, as well as to ensure that the surface layer of the workpiece has the desired quality. This purpose should be achieved in the most economical way.

Therefore, the main development trends in the field of machining by cutting and by erosion are:

(1) Reduction of material losses and this concerns both the machined materials and the tools. In connection with this aim there arises the task of reducing the machining allowances to the limits of a theoretical minimum, determined by the thickness of surface layer damaged by the preceding technological process (e.g. casting crust) and the probable dimensional errors. The problem of reducing the wear of cutting tools and eroders (the tools applied in erosion processes) also plays its part.

(2) Improvement of the quality of machined products. This means in particular the attainment of the necessary accuracy of shape and dimensions, as well as the optimization of surface layer properties from the point of view of the intended use of the product.

(3) Raising of the output and reduction of the labor consumption by the improvement of machining process, work safety and comfort. The task of mechanization and automation belongs here, especially the introduction of program controlled machining. A higher degree of mechanization and automation means higher consumption of energy. Thus there arises the problem of rational and economical use of energy, in particular electrical energy. This problem becomes acute in the case of processes consuming large amounts of energy, such as the erosion processes.

(4) The widening of machining possibilities. This requires, on the one hand, the improvement of the machinability of materials and, on the other hand, the development of new methods of machining and improvement of the existing ones, as well as the optimization of machining conditions.

The science of metal cutting and erosion should create the theoretical basis for production engineering. In this process the main development trends should be followed and the most advantageous economical solutions should be aimed at.

Words and Expressions

discharge [dis'tʃɑ:dʒ]　　　　释放
die [dai]　　　　冲模，压模
injection [in'dʒekʃən]　　　　注射，注射剂，喷射，注入资金

Unit 11　Nontraditional Machining Processes

forge	[fɔːdʒ]	锻造
electrochemical	[i‚lektrəu'kemikəl]	电化学的
anode	['ænəud]	正极，阳极
fragile	['frædʒil]	脆的，易碎的
amperage	[æm'pɛəridʒ]	安培数，电流量
ultrasonic	[‚ʌltrə'sɔnik]	超声的，超音波的
allowance	[ə'lauəns]	加工留量，容差，准许
optimization	[‚ɔptimai'zeiʃən]	最优化，最佳化
mechanization	[‚mekənai'zeiʃən]	加工性能
limit … to		局限于
in connection with		与……有关
from the point of view of		从……的观点(角度)来看
in the case of		就……来说
on (the) one hand …, on the other hand …		一方面…… 另一方面……
mold	[məuld]	铸模，塑模
pulsate	['pʌlseit]	脉动，搏动
stamp	[stæmp]	冲压
cathode	['kæθəud]	负极，阴极
electrolyte	[i'lektrəu‚lait]	电解液
voltage	['vəultidʒ]	电压(量)，伏(特)数
dissolve	[di'zɔlv]	溶解，解散，分解
erosion	[i'rəuʒən]	腐蚀，冲蚀，侵蚀
capable of		能够做
short out		短路

Notes

(1) The EDM process is valued for its ability to machine complex shapes in metals of any hardness.

is valued 在此为被动语态。由于科技文章着重描述的是客观事物和进行过程，因而常采用被动语态来侧重说明动作的承受者，或表明动作的执行者不重要，不明确，只说明了动作的承受者，而不需说明动作的执行或发出者。

本句可以翻译为：EDM 工艺的价值在于能够在任何硬度的金属上加工复杂的形状。

(2) In ultrasonic machining, also called impact grinding, fine abrasive particles suspended in a fluid (usually water) are pumped into a gap between the workpiece and the tool.

句子中 fine 的普通英语词义为"美好的，优良的"，在机械专业词汇中指的是"微小的，细小的"。

本句可以翻译为：在超声波切削(亦称冲击磨削)时，渗入某种液体(通常是水)的微细磨粒被泵进工件和刀具之间的间隙。

(3) This means in particular the attainment of the necessary accuracy of shape and dimensions, as well as the optimization of surface layer properties from the point of view of the intended use of the product.

in particular 在此指的是"特别，尤其是"，from the point of view 在此译为"从……的观点(角度)来看"。

本句可以翻译为：这特别是指如何使产品的形状和尺寸达到必要精确度，以及从产品使用角度上体现的表面层性能优化。

(4) nontraditional Machining Processes

non-：表示"否定"。

nontraditional 在此表示"非传统的，非常规的"。

诸如此类的例子还有：

parallel 平行的——nonparallel 非平行的

intersect 相交，交叉——nonintersect 非交叉

astronaut 宇航员——nonastronaut 非宇航员

另外还有类似的构词法，如：

① "re-"：表示"再次"

place 放置——replace 替换

view 观察，观看——review 回顾，复习

form 形成——reform 改造

② "over-"：表示"超过"，"过度"

load 负荷，负载——overload 超载，负荷过多

estimate 估计——overestimate 过高估计

time 时间——overtime 超时的

Exercises

1. Comprehension questions.

(1) Electrical discharge machining can be used only to machine those materials which_____.

A. conduct electricity

B. are easily broken

C. are dedicate

D. are easily shaped

(2) When a thin and fragile metal workpiece is to be machined, it is best to choose processes_____.

A. EDM, ECM or USM

B. ECM, USM or LBM

C. USM, LBM or EDM

D. LBM, ECM or EDM

(3) Tool wear is high in ultrasonic machining because of the_____.

A. ultrasonic vibration

B. abrasive operation

C. high velocity

D. fluid

(4) EDM, ECM, USM, and LBM processes have one common feature, that is: _____.

A. all of them use a kind of liquid

B. all of them are ideal for hole-drilling

C. all of them involve high tool wear

D. all of them involve no tool pressure

(5) The accurate shape and dimensions of the workpiece are connected with _____.

A. the economical way

B. the quality of the workpiece

C. the development trends

D. the surface layer of the workpiece

(6) Materials losses involve _____.

A. machined materials and the tools

B. machining allowances and theoretical minimum

C. surface layer damage and technological process

D. the wear of cutting tools and eroders

(7) Which of the following is true about mechanization and automation? _____

A. The higher the output is achieved, the lower the labor consumption is.

B. Mechanization and automation are more economical energy consumption.

C. The higher degree of mechanization and automation, the higher consumption of labor and energy.

D. Mechanization and automation reduce labor consumption but increase energy consumption.

(8) All the following are mentioned as the main development trends in the passage EXCEPT _____.

A. Reducing the labor consumption and raising the output

B. Improving the quality of the products

C. Creating the theoretical basis for production engineering

D. Reducing material losses

2. Translate the following sentences into Chinese.

(1) It is known to every machinist that on standard machine tools electrical energy is converted by an electric motor.

(2) The tool is made to vibrate a few hundredths of a millimeter at ultrasonic frequencies ranging from 19 kHz to 25 kHz.

(3) Two types of lasers are now in common use: (1)solid lasers, which are capable only of providing short bursts of power, and (2) gas lasers, which produce a continuous laser beam.

(4) In connection with this aim there arises the task of reducing the machining allowances to

the limits of a theoretical minimum, determined by the thickness of surface layer damaged by the preceding technological process (e.g. casting crust)and the probable dimensional errors.

3. Translate the following phrases into English.

(1) 铸模

(2) 冲模

(3) 锻造

(4) 冲压

(5) 电化学的

(6) 溶解

(7) 局限于

(8) 与……有关

(9) 从……的观点(角度)来看

(10) 就……来说

4. Translate the following phrases into Chinese according to the text.

(1) electrical discharge machining

(2) electrochemical machining

(3) ultrasonic machining

(4) laser beam machining

(5) short out

(6) in particular

(7) standard machine tools

(8) dimensional errors

5. Write a 100-word summary according to the text.

课文参考译文

第 11 单元　非传统加工工艺

非传统加工工艺也称为"特种加工工艺"或"现代加工工艺"，泛指用电能、热能、光能、电化学能、化学能、声能及特殊机械能等能量达到去除或增加材料的加工方法，从而实现材料被去除、变形、改变性能或被镀覆等。本单元主要介绍了电火花加工(EDM)、电化学加工(ECM)、超声加工(USM)、激光加工(LBM)和切削与腐蚀加工的发展趋势。

11.1　电火花加工

EDM 通过刀具与工件之间的受控电弧(火花)进行金属切削。EDM 工艺的价值在于能够在任何硬度的金属上加工复杂的形状，广泛用来制造橡胶和塑料注塑模和压塑模，压铸金属模，以及金属锻压模和冲模。由于刀具不施压力，因此是切削易碎材料的理想工艺。

每一个机工(或机械师)都知道，在通用机床上，电能通过电动机转换成运动。近来，我们发现，电能能够直接用来切削金属。其主要优点是：用电加工法能够加工任何硬度的金属，而且表面粗糙度值小。

电火花加工是一种切除金属的方式。在此过程中，脉动直流电通到成形刀具(电极)和工件，两者都能导电。刀具和工件靠得很近，其间有不导电的液体用来绝缘。当电压高到足以击穿这一绝缘体时，火花就跳过刀具和工件之间的间隙。于是，这一火花就切除了少量的金属(见图11-1)。

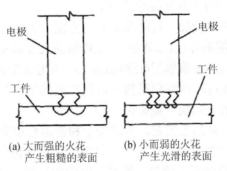

(a) 大而强的火花产生粗糙的表面
(b) 小而弱的火花产生光滑的表面

图 11-1 电火花加工过程

电火花机床加工零件的表面粗糙度值的大小取决于工件和电极之间所产生的火花的大小。图 11-1 表明，大而强的火花产生粗糙的表面；小而弱的火花产生光滑的表面。据报道，金属切除的速度和表面粗糙度是由火花的频率和强度控制的。频率高、强度低的火花，导致金属切削速度低，而表面粗糙度值小；频率低、强度高的火花，导致金属切削速度快，但表面粗糙度值高。

11.2 电化学加工

在电化学加工时，刀具是正极，工具是负极。刀具与工件之间留有 0.0254mm 至 0.76mm 的间隙。电解液可在这一间隙中流动，并保持电路联通。低压、高安培的直流电流通过电解液从工件传输到刀具。通过电化反应，电流把工件上的金属粒子熔进电解液。ECM 工艺可用来切削一切导电的金属，不论其硬度如何。由于工件上不受压力，ECM 是切削薄型金属和易损工件的理想工艺。

11.3 超声波加工

在超声波加工(亦称冲击磨削)时，渗入某种液体(通常是水)的微细磨粒被泵进工件和刀具之间的间隙。刀具以 19 000 Hz 至 25 000 Hz 的超声频率作百分之几毫米的振动。刀具的快速泵射带动磨粒高速喷向工件，从而把工件磨削成为刀具的形状。USM 的一个主要优点是可以切削不导电的材料，也就是 EDM 或 ECM 工艺不能加工的材料。但是，由于 USM 是磨削加工，因而刀具损耗大。要加工一个工件，通常需要一个或多个粗加工刀具和一个精加工刀具。由冷压钢或不锈钢制成的刀具耐磨效果最佳。

11.4 激光加工

激光加工的能量来源于一束高聚焦光。当光束在一个小点上聚焦时，其功率强度得以提高，并产生足够的热量来汽化任何材料。不过，由于金属切削量很少，使得激光切削的应用局限于钻孔和较薄材料的切削。通常使用的激光器有两种：①只能发出短促脉冲的固体激光器；②能发出不间断激光束的气体激光器。

11.5 切削与腐蚀加工的发展趋势

切削与腐蚀加工的目的是将工件加工成所需的形状并达到必要精确度的尺寸，同时还要确保工件表面层的质量要求。这一目的还应以最经济的方法去达到。

因此，切削与腐蚀加工的主要发展趋势如下。

(1) 减少材料浪费，这涉及加工材料和刀具两方面。为达到这一目的，就必须根据上道工序加工所破坏的表面层的厚度(如铸层)以及可能的尺寸误差，将加工留量减少至理论上的最小范围。减少切削刀具和腐蚀器(在腐蚀加工中所用的工具)的损耗同样也很重要。

(2) 提高加工产品的质量。这特别是指如何使产品的形状和尺寸达到必要精确度，以及从产品使用角度上体现的表面层性能优化。

(3) 提高产量并通过改善加工工艺、劳动安全和舒适程度来减少劳力消耗。机械化和自动化的任务在此特指程序控制加工的引进。机械化和自动化的程度越高，耗能就越大。由此就产生了如何合理和经济利用能量，特别是电能的问题。这一问题在耗能较大的生产中(如腐蚀加工)尤为突出。

(4) 扩大加工范围。一方面要改进材料的可加工性，另一方面要开发出新的加工方法并对现行方法进行改进，同时还要优化加工条件。

对金属切削和腐蚀加工的研究应为生产工艺提供理论基础。在这一过程中，应该跟上主要的发展趋势，寻求最有利的经济加工方法。

Technical Reading

Metal Cutting

Metal cutting, commonly called machining, is the removal of the unwanted metal from a workpiece in the form of chips so as to obtain a finished product of desired size, shape, and finish. United States industries annually spend $60 billion to perform metal removal operations because the vast majority of manufactured products require machining at some stage in their production, ranging from relatively rough or nonprecision work, such as cleanup of castings or forgings, to high-precision work involving tolerances of 0.0001 inch or less. Thus, machining undoubtedly is the most important of the basic manufacturing processes.

Machines for metal cutting are called machine tools. Workpieces are held in the workholding device. A cutting tools used to machine the metal.

The properties of the work material are important in chip formation. High-strength materials require larger forces than materials of lower strength, causing greater tool and work deflection and increased friction, heat generation, and operating temperatures, and requiring greater work input. The structure and composition also influence metal cutting. Hard or abrasive constituents, such as carbides in steel, accelerate tool wear.

Unit 12   Dialogue Practice

China International Machine Tool Show (CIMT) is China's largest international machine tool exhibition, sponsored by the China machine tool industry association. CIMT is one of the four most important machine tool exhibitions in the world. It has been held in China every 2 years ever since its existence in 1989. It has made great achievements since 1989, and it also consolidate and enhance china's position in the field of international machine tool. Engineers and managers from all parts of the world flock to Beijing, where they get abreast of the latest manufacturing technology and promote their new products. Also, you may find job opportunities here.

Shi Jun, a salesman of a machine tool building manufacture

Smith, a foreign businessman

12.1   Outside the Exhibition Hall

Shi: Nice to meet you! I'm Shi Jun. What's your name please?

Smith: Nice to meet you, too! I'm Smith.

Shi: You are welcome to the eleventh session of China International Machine Tool Show. The opening ceremony is being performed now.

Smith: Yes, the scene is lively. How long will the CIMT'2009 last?

Shi: It will last for 6 days from today to April 11, 2009.

Smith: Very good. It seems to be a big show.

Shi: Exactly. According to statistics, 1200 exhibitors from 28 countries and regions participate in CIMT'2009.

Smith: I'm lucky to have this opportunity to participate in CIMT'2009.

Shi: You are right. The show has been very important to China's machine tool industry. There are more than 1200 new machine tools on display.

Smith: Fantastic! Do you have such a big show every year?

Shi: It has been held in China every 2 years ever since its existence in 1989. And the show has been recognized as one of the top four marketing activities in the world's machine tool arena.

Smith: I'm sure to come next time.

Shi: Very good. You are welcome!

12.2   Inside the Exhibition Hall

Smith: Look! How spectacular the exhibits are!

Shi: Of course. Here on display are some new homemade machine tools. Many of them have caught up with the technical levels of similar products made abroad. Let me show you around.

Smith: It's very kind of you! Oh, that's a big simultaneous six-axis CNC machine.

Shi: Yes. This is a new machine which reaches the advanced world level. It is suitable for air industry.

Smith: I see. Is this a boring-milling machine?

Shi: Yes. That's right. It is highly recommended in the world because it is economical, easy to operate and outstanding in performance.

Smith: That sounds interesting. But the size is a bit small.

Shi: It is specially designed for small works, and it is stable and efficient. The bigger one is also available. Over there, you see.

Smith: What's the unit price?

Shi: Here is our price list and this is the catalogue.

12.3　In the Negotiation Booth

Smith: We have studied your catalogue and we have great interest in your boring-milling machine. But your price has been found higher through repeated calculations.

Shi: How many would you like to order?

Smith: Our quantity is surely to your satisfaction. We plan to order 20 if the price is moderate.

Shi: To be frank, such machine was out of stock for a while because we had too many orders. The price on the list now is the same as it was before. But since your order has a size, we would like to have another new partner by reducing the unit price to $22 000 FOB Shanghai. That's our bottom price.

Smith: It seems acceptable. When can you make goods ready for shipment?

Shi: Around September.

Smith: Well, we expect to use them this November. Time is too tight. We need to transit the goods at Singapore since there is no direct steamer from Shanghai to Lagos. Could you get the goods ready for shipment in late August.

Shi: August is OK.

Smith: When can we sign the contract?

Shi: Tomorrow morning.

Smith: See you tomorrow then.

Shi: See you tomorrow.

Words and Expressions

opportunity　　[ˌɔpə'tjuːniti]　　　　　机会

delegation	[ˌdeliˈgeiʃən]	表团，展团
exhibit	[igˈzibit]	展品
spectacular	[spekˈtækjulə]	壮观的
negotiation	[niˌgəuʃiˈeiʃən]	谈判
booth	[bu:θ]	展位
catalogue	[ˈkætəlɔ:g]	产品样本，目录
order	[ˈɔ:də]	订货，订购
moderate	[ˈmɔdərit]	适中的
steamer	[ˈsti:mə]	船
shipment	[ˈʃipmənt]	装船，交货
contract	[ˈkɔntrækt]	合同
transit	[ˈtrænsit]	运输
bottom price		最低价
opening ceremony		开幕式
exhibition hall		展览馆，展览厅
homemade machine tool		国产机床
simultaneous six-axis CNC machine		六轴联动数控机床
boring-milling machine		铣镗床
unit price		单价
out of stock		脱销
have a size		订货达到一定数量
Lagos		拉各斯，尼日利亚首都
direct steamer		直达航运
sign the contract		签订合同
Free on Board (FOB)		离岸价

Notes

(1) CIMT is one of the four most important machine tool exhibitions in the world.

CIMT 是 China International Machine Tool 的缩写，代表中国国际机床展览会。中国国际机床展览会，是中国最大的国际机床工具展览会，由中国机床工具工业协会主办。它得到中国政府的批准和支持。从 1989 年起(逢单年)举行一次，已取得了巨大成就，受到海内外的好评，被国际同行誉为世界四大国际机床展之一。其他国际机床展览会分别在美国、欧洲和日本举行。第十一届中国国际机床展览会 CIMT'2009 在北京于 2009 年 4 月 6 日至 11 日举行。

本句可以翻译为：中国国际机床展览会是世界四大机床展览会之一。

(2) Engineers and managers from all parts of the world flock to Beijing, where they get abreast of the latest manufacturing technology and promote their new products.

flock 一般意思是"人群，群众"，在此做动词，表示"云集，集合"。

get abreast of 在此意思是"获得……，跟上……"。

where 在此引导一个定语从句，指代的是 Beijing。

本句可以翻译为：世界各国的工程师和经理云集北京，了解世界制造技术新动态，推广最先进的机床制造产品。

(3) But since your order has a size, we would like to have another new partner by reducing the unit price to $20,000 FOB Shanghai.

FOB 在此为 Free on Board 的简写，意思是"离岸价"。

unit price 在此可以翻译为"单价"。

本句可以翻译为：但是，考虑到你们的订单有一定的量，我们把单价降到上海离岸价 22 000 美元，这样我们可以成为新的合作伙伴。

Exercises

1. Answer the following questions according to the text above.

(1) What is the full name for CIMT?

(2) How many people came to the CIMT'2009?

(3) Why did so many people come to CIMT?

(4) How many new machine tools were there on display at CIMT?

2. Comprehension questions.

(1) Where did the CIMT hold in the text? _____
A. Beijing   B. Shanghai   C. Lagos   D. Singapore

(2) How many machine tools did Smith plan to order?_____
A. 10   B. 15   C. 20   D. 25

(3) How many exhibitors participated in CIMT'2009? _____
A. 1000   B. 1200   C. 1500   D. 2800

(4) When would the machine tools ordered by Smith be expected to use?_____
A. November   B. August   C. October   D. September

3. Translate the following sentences into Chinese.

(1) China International Machine Tool Show (CIMT) is China's largest international machine tool exhibition, sponsored by the China machine tool industry association.

(2) Many of them have caught up with the technical levels of similar products made abroad. Let me show you around.

(3) It is highly recommended in the world because it is economical, easy to operate and outstanding in performance.

(4) To be frank, such machine was out of stock for a while because we had too many orders.

(5) We need to transit the goods at Singapore since there is no direct steamer from Shanghai to Lagos.

Unit 12 Dialogue Practice

4. Translate the following phrases into English.

(1) 最低价

(2) 六轴联动数控机床

(3) 直达航运

(4) 离岸价

(5) 展览馆，展览厅

(6) 脱销

(7) 签订合同

5. Translate the following phrases into Chinese according to the text.

(1) opening ceremony

(2) homemade machine tool

(3) boring-milling machine

(4) unit price

(5) have a size

(6) sign the contract

(7) flock to

(8) the latest manufacturing technology

6. Write a 80-word summary according to the text.

课文参考译文

第 12 单元 对话练习

中国国际机床展览会(CIMT)是中国最大的国际机床工具展览会，由中国机床工具工业协会主办。中国国际机床展览会是世界四大机床展览会之一。自从 1989 年第一届中国国际机床展览会以来，在中国每两年举行一次。它从第一次展览会以来取得了巨大的成就，同时也进一步巩固和提高了中国在国际机床领域的地位。世界各国的工程师和经理云集北京，了解世界制造技术新动态，推广最先进的机床制造产品。同时，在这种展览会中你也许会发现一些工作机会。

石军：机床生产厂家的销售员。

史密斯：外国商人。

12.1 展馆外……

石军：　你好！我叫石军，请问您尊姓大名？

史密斯：见到你很高兴，我叫史密斯。

石军：　欢迎来到北京参加第十一届中国国际机床展览会。现在正在举行的是本届展览会的开幕仪式。

史密斯：是的，这个场面真热闹啊！CIMT 将持续几天呢？

石军： CIMT 将从今天开始持续到 2009 年 4 月 11 日，一共 6 天。

史密斯： 不错啊，看起来是一个大展览会啊。

石军： 对啊。据统计，有来自 28 个国家和地区的 1200 余家厂商参展。

史密斯： 我感到很荣幸能有这次机会参加这次展览会。

石军： 你说得对。本次展览会对于中国的机床工业来说意义重大。有 1200 多台新机床参加本次的展览会。

史密斯： 太棒了，你们每年都有这样的展会吗？

石军： 自从 1989 年第一届中国国际机床展览会以来，中国每两年举行一次。该展览会被公认为是世界机床领域四大展销活动之一。

史密斯： 下次我肯定会来的。

石军： 太好了，欢迎你的到来。

12.2 展馆内……

史密斯： 你看，这次的展品好壮观啊！

石军： 那当然啦。这里展出的是一些国产新机床，其中很多已经赶上国外同类产品的技术水平。我带你到处参观转转。

史密斯： 你真是太好了！哟，那儿是一台大型六轴联动数控机床。

石军： 是的。这台机床达到了世界先进水平，适用于航空工业。

史密斯： 这是铣镗床吗？

石军： 对，由于它经济实用、操作简便、性能优良，在世界上很畅销。

史密斯： 很有意思，就是机床尺寸小了点。

石军： 它专为小工件设计，稳定性好，效率高。大一点的也有，你看，在那儿。

史密斯： 单价多少？

石军： 这是我们的价格表，这是产品样本。

12.3 在谈判间……

史密斯： 我们已经看过你们的样本，对你们的铣镗床很感兴趣。但通过反复计算发现价格高了一点。

石军： 你们想要订多少台？

史密斯： 我们的数量肯定让你满意。如果价格合适，我们计划订 20 台。

石军： 说实话，由于我们订单太多，这种机床已经销售一空了。现在价格表和以前是一样的。但是，考虑到你们的订单有一定的量，我们把单价降到上海离岸价 22 000 美元，这样我们可以成为新的合作伙伴。那是我们的底价。

史密斯： 看起来可以接受。什么时候交货？

石军： 9 月份左右。

史密斯： 我们希望是在今年 11 月份使用这些机床。时间非常紧迫，由于从上海到拉各斯没有直达航运，我们要把机床运到新加坡中转，8 月末能交货吗？

石军： 8 月可以。

史密斯： 我们什么时候签订合同？

石军： 明天上午见。

史密斯：明天见！

石军：　明天见！

Technical Reading

Interview

Place: Personnel Manager's Office in a company

Characters: (interviewer) Mike Anderson, Personnel Manager of a company

(Applicant) Wangjian

I: Come in, please. Good morning, I am Mike Anderson, personnel manager of our company.

A: How do you do? My name is Wangjian.

I: Sit down please and make yourself at home.

A: Thank you very much.

I: As I know you have applied to work in our company. Would you introduce yourself, please?

A: I'm 24 years old and was born in Beijing. There are three members in my family: father, mother, and I.

I: That's good. What about your educational background?

A: I can speak and write English fluently as shown in the resume and know how to operate the computer and NC machines. I have been an assistant engineer for half a year in a famous company one year ago. So, I am sure that I am quite efficient in technical work, like NC programming, operation, maintenance and debugging.

I: OK, I would infer that you are an excellent student in your college. Could you tell me the courses you have learned in your college?

A: I have learned many courses. English, Mathematics, Engineering Drawing, Mechanical Engineering, C-Language Program Designing, Electric and Electronics, and so on, are the basic courses we learnt during the first two years. Especially, English takes much time in my Industrial and Commercial Foreign Languages College. Additionally, I have learned many specialized courses. Such as Machining Processes and Metal Cutting, Hydraulic Drive, Electromechanical Control, NC Programming and Operation, CAD/CAM, 3DMAX, Internet, Electronic-Commerce, Economics, Trade and so on.

I: I am very interested in your major and English courses. Can you tell me more details about them?

A: All right. Though I am a student in the Department of Mechanical and Electrical Engineering, I studied many English courses including English Reading and Comprehension, Oral English, English Writing and Professional English. Most of the courses are taught in English, some are even taught by foreign teachers.

I: By the way, do you have any experience as a leader at the school?

A: Yes, I was the monitor of our class in the first two years. I have organized many social activities. Also, I have been the chairman of the students' union in the second two years. I am pleased to take part in all kinds of social activities. Such experience gave me a lot of confidence in my ability to see through things.

    I: Besides all these, what do you like to do in your spare time?

    A: I have a great interest in travel, reading and sports such as swimming, tennis and so on.

    I: I am very glad to hear that. Travel and sports are also my hobbies. We have discussed a lot about you since the beginning of our interview. We'd better shift to other topics. Why do you choose our company?

    A: Your company is one of the largest NC machine manufacturers in East China. As you see in my resume, I specialized in CAD/CAM in college, so I expect to develop my capabilities in your company. On the other hand, the position for which I applied is quite challenging. That's the reason why I like to come to your company. I hope to display my talents fully here.

    I: If I accept you, how much do you expect to be paid?

    A: At least ￥1500 a month.

    I: That will be no problem.

    A: Could I ask you some other questions?

    I: Certainly. I am glad to answer them.

    A: Do you provide housing and what about work hours?

    I: Well. Our company doesn't provide any housing. There are 8 regular hours a day. In general, it is from 8:30 a.m. to 5:00 p.m., extra work may be required sometimes with payment and someone need to be on duty on Saturday or Sunday without payment.

    A: I wonder what qualities you look for in the person who is to fill the position.

    I: First of all, he must have a strong sense of responsibility and secondly he must also be diligent and do a lot of things on his own initiative. Finally he should have a wide range of knowledge.

    A: OK. When can I get the reply about my application?

    I: I think you will know the final result within a week. It's my pleasure to have a talk with you.

    A: Me too. It takes you much time. Goodbye.

    I: Goodbye.

参 考 文 献

[1] 蒋忠理. 机电与数控专业英语[M]. 北京：机械工业出版社，2004.
[2] P. N. Rao. Manufacturing Technology—Metal cutting and Machine Tools[M]. 北京：机械工业出版社，2003.
[3] Herbert W. Wsge. Manufacturing Engineering [M]. MI: Society of Manufacturing Engineers, 1994.
[4] 汤彩萍. 数控技术专业英语[M]. 北京：电子工业出版社，2007.
[5] 李桂云. 数控技术专业英语[M]. 大连：大连铁道出版社，2008.
[6] 刘瑛等. 数控技术英语[M]. 北京：化学工业出版社，2003.
[7] 李鹏飞. 机电专业英语[M]. 北京：高等教育出版社，2011.
[8] 戴正阳. 机电专业英语[M]. 北京：北京大学出版社，2011.
[9] 谭雪松，杨财容. 机电专业英语[M]. 北京：人民邮电出版社，2010.
[10] 卜养玲. 数控专业英语[M]. 北京：北京理工大学出版社，2010.
[11] 施平. 机械工程专业英语教程[M]. 北京：电子工业出版社，2012.
[12] 伍忠杰. 机械专业英语[M]. 北京：北京理工大学出版社，1996.
[13] 李光布. 机械工程专业英语[M]. 武汉：华中科技大学出版社，2009.
[14] www.toolingu.com
[15] www.cncci.com